DOGS

YANN ARTHUS-BERTRAND

DOGS
YANN ARTHUS-BERTRAND

TEXTS BY

ANDRÉ PITTION-ROSSILLON

TRANSLATION BY

JOHN HERRICK

BARNES
&NOBLE
BOOKS
NEW YORK

*I dedicate this book to all those who were
kind and patient enough to come to my studio,
whether they do or do not appear in the book.
Thank you.*

PREFACE

Dogs have been a close part of mankind's life since our earliest days. As hunters, then watchdogs, sheepdogs, protectors and companions, they have chosen man just as much as man has chosen them. Each dog finds a certain sense of fulfillment performing the numerous tasks that are characteristic of its specific breed—and each breed is clearly differentiated as a result of centuries of selective breeding.

As they have a long history by our side, dogs exist only with man and through man in a bond of trust and complicity. It therefore seemed natural when Yann Arthus-Bertrand decided to depict the master and dog together. The sensitivity, the precise tone and the joy experienced by the photographer during the shoots mean that the readers of this book will enjoy the pleasure of emotion tinged with humor.

By prefacing *Dogs,* I feel I am perpetuating the tradition of those who set up the French Central Canine Society (CCS) one hundred and ten years ago. Scrupulous work has meant that good representatives of some two hundred and thirty breeds have been depicted.

This beautiful book, the fruit of a spontaneous idea, is also the result of teamwork. I would here like to hail my friend André Pittion-Rossillon, who wrote the texts, and to thank the breeders and owners who appear in this book for their wholehearted participation. I should also like to acknowledge the hard work of the secretaries of the CCS.

Thus, it is in order better to feel and understand the harmony that reigns between mankind and dogs that I have the pleasure of inviting you to enjoy this book.

Camille Michel
President of the French Central Canine Society

CONTENTS

INTRODUCTION

Dogs were the first animals domesticated by man. This occurred ten thousand years ago, when the two formed an alliance that enabled them to win the terrible combat for survival. Their success together gradually encouraged the dog to accept man's authority. During the following centuries, their relationship continued to deepen, thanks to the increasingly varied tasks dogs were given. From boundless trust, it grew into such a profound friendship that dogs now share fully in the joys and woes of the households in which they are members.

As a dog lover, Yann Arthus-Bertrand has always been fascinated by the extraordinary quality of the relationships between dogs and members of their families. This prompted him to produce a book that would depict the way dogs display their affection for their masters. He also wanted this book to help those who wished to acquire a dog to choose the companion best-suited to their lifestyle. He thus naturally turned to the French Central Canine Society, which has been working since 1882 to improve all the breeds in France, with a request for short texts as commentaries for his photographs of each breed. All of the world's recognized breeds are listed in the Society's inventory, which has been adopted by the Belgium-based World Canine Organization (also known as the Fédération Cynologique Internationale), which was created in the early 1930s to develop a coherent policy concerning dog shows and dog breeding.

The breeds are classified into ten groups, according to their physical characteristics, geographical origins and natural dispositions. This classification has been used to structure this book because, by indicating the characteristics shared by all members of a group at the beginning of each section, long and tedious repetitions have been avoided.

The photos are amusing, moving surprising and indicative of the special relationship between people and their dogs. Each of them is accompanied by a short text containing additional information and anecdotes.

HERDERS: SHEEPDOGS AND CATTLE DOGS

As early as prehistoric times, mankind noticed that dogs instinctively herded animals together. At first, shepherds simply took advantage of this instinct. Soon, though, they needed dogs that could help them and were adapted to the specific weather conditions and terrain where they kept their flocks or herds. By using pragmatic and carefully monitored selective breeding techniques, they created many breeds of sheepdog.

A herder's work consists of two distinct tasks. The first involves taking the flock to pastures or to the pen. The dog must make certain that the sheep move in an orderly manner to facilitate the transfer. It will keep its charges on the side of the road, then form them into a line when they must cross some obstacle (such as a narrow passage, bridges, gates and so on). The dog's second job is to keep a permanent watch over the flock when it has reached the pasture, to keep the animals within their appointed limits and bring back any strays.

This demanding work requires extremely diverse capacities, notably energy, intelligence, courage, discernment and rapid reflexes. A sheepdog must also be very fit, for its job requires it to cover a considerable distance each day (from 24 to 42 miles). Finally, it must have an excellent visual memory, should only bark when strictly necessary and never bite.

With the development of technological farming, shepherds made less use of their dogs. Given the wide range of skills they had learned from their previous employment, herders are today used for new forms of work: as watchdogs, searching for missing persons, detection of drugs and explosives, as guide-dogs for the blind and assistance for the disabled. It is also interesting to note that over the last few years farmers have begun to use herders again. While in the past they used to entrust them with just one species, the dogs are now expected to herd cattle, sheep, pigs and poultry.

Herders form the first group in the international classification of dog breeds. This group is divided into two subgroups: the first, "sheepdogs," contains all of those breeds used by farmers for the daily maneuvering and supervision of livestock; the second, "cattle dogs," includes the breeds previously used by wholesale butchers to drive herds of animals to slaughterhouses. All the dogs in the first group are still used in their traditional tasks. The separation into two subgroups has been maintained because of the morphological differences due to the original use of these dogs.

Swiss cattle dogs are not included in the second subgroup because they are primarily mountain dogs, and are thus listed with their fellows in the second group.

BELGIAN SHEEPDOG

This breed descended from various local sheepdogs that were grouped together in 1891 by Professor Reul, who held the zoology chair at the Veterinary School of Brussels. This grouping allowed him to find four dogs with the same morphology, differing only in the nature and color of their fur.

This elegant, robust, well-proportioned dog is made to withstand inclement weather and atmospheric variations. Like the German shepherd, its ability to adapt means that it can be used for various tasks. It is about 25 inches tall, with a long head with small upright triangular ears, a slightly elongated neck and a powerful yet agile body. Vigilant and attentive, its lively, questioning stare reveals a great intelligence. It has lightning reflexes. Always on the move, it never seems to tire. It must be trained young with patience and kindness, but also with a firm hand. It requires a lot of exercise to burn off its natural energy.

MALINOIS

Its face is black, and its short fur is a black-flecked fawn color. Exuberant and impetuous, Barox du Mas des Lavandes expresses his pleasure in carrying out the tasks that Guy Lamotte gives him by leaping into his master's arms, especially after participating in a competition.

TERVUEREN

This breed has a long black-flecked
fawn or buff coat.
Elda du Bois des Tôt and her four
puppies belong to Mrs. Chantal
Jouannet.

LAEKENOIS

Of the four varieties of Belgian shepherds, this one has the fewest dogs. Its coat is rough, fawn-colored and tousled.

Mr. Claude Adjadj's two Laekenoises closely observe his slightest gesture or movement. The male, for example, noticed that his master turned a key in a lock to open doors, and tried to imitate him. He gripped the key in his teeth and shook his head to make it turn—but so vigorously that the key broke in the lock.

As for the female, Undine de l'Orchidée Noire, Mr. Adjadj regrets not having trusted her instinct when, upon leaving an exhibition in Belgium, he noticed that he had lost his wallet containing his iden-

tity papers. Feeling irritable, he stopped Undine from trying to crawl underneath a nearby vehicle, pushed her into his car and drove back to France. That night, the man who had been parked next to him rang him up to inform him that he had found his wallet under the car, and that his identity papers were safe in the Netherlands. If he had followed Undine's indications, he would have saved himself the 540-mile trip he had to make to recover his papers.

GROENENDAEL

This variety has a characteristic coat of long, completely black fur. Vulcain du Château des Mousseaux and Doria du Castel d'Argences belong to Jean-Michel Auvray, and are excellent examples of this breed.

SCHIPPERKE

During the Middle Ages, peasants often entrusted their flocks to the breed in its native Flanders. This small, lively black Belgian devil still possesses all of the qualities of a good sheepdog. With its pointed snout and small triangular ears, it looks somthing like a fox. It has a stocky neck, broad chest and straight back. Its abundant and resistant fur forms a beautiful black coat. The lack of a tail is characteristic. It is a rustic dog and easy to keep. Vigorous, agile and tireless, it constantly observes what is happening around it. It enjoys the company of horses. What is more, it is a good mole hunter. It should not be forgotten that it needs a lot of exercise despite its small size.

To be as content as Mrs. Pierre Marlière's two dogs, the Schipperke should receive a solid but calm education. Be-Bop du Parc de l'Haÿ is six and has successfully passed a natural capacity test, which evaluates a Schipperke's ability to remain calm under pressure.

PICARDY SHEEPDOG

This is the dog that accompanied the Celts when they left southwest Germany to invade Gaul. It is average-sized, rustic yet elegant, vigorous, muscular and well built. Its face is intelligent and lively. Its medium-length wiry coat is like a Griffon terrier's. Its head is well proportioned, its neck strong and muscular and its back straight. Its coat varies from a fawn to grayish black, including all the intermediary shades, but its wiry fur, which is harsh to the touch, is never white, black, or white and black.

Spontaneous and pleasant, it can be trained easily with firm but not brutal treatment. Speaking loudly is usually sufficient. It is naturally very protective of children and its master, as is shown by Vanille and Annette, both ready to react if anybody shows any aggression toward Vincent Diard.

BRIARD

This old French breed is a sheepdog of the plains, and its origin has never been clearly identified. Some dog specialists think it is a distant descendent of the prehistoric dog of the peat bogs, while others claim that this longhaired sheepdog came from a cross between a Barbet and a Beauce shepherd.

It is longer than it is tall, and its rather elongated head is covered with long hair forming a moustache, beard and eyebrows which partly mask its eyes. Its ears are straight, its chest broad, its back straight and its rear quarters slightly curved. Its long coat looks like goat fur and requires vigorous brushing. Rustic, muscular, supple and well proportioned, it has a lively and alert appearance. Though expansive in its expressions of affection for its masters, it also enjoys lying calmly beside them, like Lukas de L'Hermitrie with Mrs. Peggy Jacoulot. But it must not be forgotten that this sporty dog needs activity and can tolerate life in an apartment or house only if it is given plenty of exercise.

BEAUCERON

This breed comes from the short-haired variety of French flatland sheepdogs that used to be found throughout France. Pierre Mégnin, one of the founders of modern cynology (the science of dog breeding), was the first to coin the term "Beauceron," simply because this breed was common in the Beauce region in 1888.

Rustic, solid and large (it measures from 26 to 28 inches), it is also well built and muscular. Its graceful shape endeared it to the writer Colette, who loved this breed. This powerful sheepdog has a long but well-proportioned head, a high broad chest, a perfectly straight back and marvelous poise. Its coat, made up of dense short hairs, is generally black and tan, though it can be harlequin (gray and black, either in equal parts or in patches). Whatever the case, all members of the breed have tan markings, particularly on the feet, which gave them the nickname of "red stockings."

The harmonious development of its potential requires firm but not brutal training. Well-behaved and enduring, it becomes extremely attached to its master, whom it identifies as the leader it has been looking for. This is the case with the sheepdogs belonging to Mr. Jacky Levilain, and especially Artus Sarah de la Mare aux Templiers, who is always by his side.

CATALAN SHEPHERD

Dringola de la Folie Myosotis and Eco, who belong to Mr. Emmanuel Thisse, have certain similarities with the French Pyrenean shepherd. This is not surprising, as the Catalan shepherd and the Pyrenean shepherd both come from an original breed imported from Tibet. With a maximum height of 22 inches, the Catalan shepherd has a solid head, with fine triangular ears. Its neck is muscular and short. Its long, solid body creates an impression of strength and agility. A mustache, beard and eyebrows, which do not mask its eyes, are formed by its stiff long hair, which can be straight or wavy. Its coat can be fawn, or else fawn speckled with black or gray. First and foremost a working dog, it really expresses its personality only when leading its flock. It gallops only on extremely open land and requires a lot of exercise. It can easily put up with the heat, cold or bad weather.

LONGHAIRED COLLIE
Collie-Rough

This breed descends from the sheepdogs that escorted the Roman legions when Caesar conquered Britain. As a specialist in leading flocks of sheep, it has established itself in Scotland, where sheep are plentiful. Official recognition of this breed greatly contributed to its renown in Great Britain, where it was admired for its figure and its elegance. The collie has thus become mainly a pet, and Scottish sheep farmers often use other breeds that have retained their original rusticity and skills. Its faithfulness was popularized in the cinema by the *Lassie* films. With its graceful, exceptionally well-proportioned figure and beautiful coat, the collie's maximum height is

24 inches. It is universally admired. The natural affection which it inspires in us is increased by the characteristic softness of its stare, as in the way Bella di Volorio is looking at Mr. Olivo. Its body is long and its back straight. The tail is long and its tip turns slightly upward. Its coat is made up of dense, straight hair that is harsh to the touch. It can be fawn or somewhat flecked, black dotted with fawn or a blue mixed with black and fawn patches. These three coats are marked with white to a greater or lesser extent.

SHORTHAIRED COLLIE
Collie-Smooth

A far less common smooth collie also exists. Astrellita Angel's Tears, sitting calmly beside Miss Deborah Palmer, could easily rival Lassie for her faithfulness. With great attention and tenderness, she watches over Miss Palmer's young nephews when they play, brings up the puppies of the house and washes the family's rabbit and hamsters.

GERMAN SHEPHERD

At the end of the nineteenth century, Germany had many breeds of sheepdogs with extremely different physical characteristics, which were to be found only in their original regions. The unification of its thirty-nine states in 1870 gave rise to a strong sense of German nationalism. This inspired Captain Von Stephanitz, a Prussian officer who was a keen cynologist, to envisage the creation of a new breed which would possess all the qualities of the various regional breeds as a symbol of a united Germany. When this had been achieved, he naturally called his new breed the "German shepherd," though it is better known to the English as the "Alsatian."

Standing 26 inches tall, with a lean head, strong snout and straight pointed ears, this dog has firm muscles, a powerful back, a well-developed frame and solid limbs. Its thick harsh fur protects it from bad weather. Its angular limbs makes it able to trot with its body near the ground and keep up its pace for a long time. This athlete needs plenty of daily exercise.

When well-trained—it needs an inflexible but fair master—it can adapt itself to any situation. It can happily carry out any of the tasks it is given. It is also a very faithful companion and good with children. When looking for his young niece Fanny, for example, Mr. Christian Starosciak found her asleep between Eleazor du Normont's paws. This three-year-old shepherd, a trained guard dog, was affectionately watching over her sleep, while remaining motionless so as not to awaken her.

BOUVIER DES FLANDRES

Originally from Franco-Belgian Flanders, this breed has the particularity of having a double nationality. It is thus managed by both France and Belgium. The disputes between dog-breeders regarding its origins are pointless. Since the breeders were decimated by the violent combats which ravaged Flanders in 1914-18 and 1939-45, the French and Belgians quite sensibly worked together to re-create the breed from a handful of specimens from different pedigrees, some of which had received new crossings at the end of the nineteenth century.

The huge appearance of its head is accentuated by its beard and mustache. Its short stocky body stands on strong muscular limbs and creates an impression of great force. Its thick coat is formed of dry matte hair, which is harsh to the touch, about 2 inches long and slightly tousled. It is generally fawn or gray, often brindled or speckled, and sometimes plain black.

Boby du Bas-Ferry proved his love for Mr. Bernard Mauroy in dramatic circumstances. While on their way to a dog show, they were in a car crash and Mr. Mauroy fainted. Boby then stood guard over his master's unconscious body until help arrived. Only then did he allow people to approach him.

YUGOSLAVIAN SHEEPDOG

This Yugoslavian sheepdog originated in the mountains of Sar Planina, which separate Kosovo from Macedonia to the north and Albania to the northeast. Measuring an average 25 inches high, it is robust, well built, with V-shaped ears that fall down onto its cheeks. Its head is well proportioned and its body powerful and rather long. Its coat, made up of long almost flat hairs, which are rather coarse, is of one color—any of the shades between white and a dark brown that verges on black. It requires almost no care. The Sarplaninac is better suited to country life than town, because it needs to use its energy in long trots, which is its favorite gait.

Mr. Gérard Millet often says that he lives with Dimitri and his partner rather than the other way round. By this provocative statement, he shows that he has trained his two Sarplaninacs so well that they have become full-fledged members of the family.

SCHAPENDOES

The origin of this longhaired Dutch sheepdog has not been precisely established. It is presumably the descendent of a small Asian dog that was crossed with regional Dutch dogs.

Measuring a maximum of 20 inches, it is rustic, well balanced and an enthusiastic worker. Its head is covered with abundant hair, while its medium-length body has long bushy hair which is fine and dry, and forms a brown, white, black or gray coat, or any of the shades between white and black.

Gentiane de la Vallée des Troglodytes, proudly sitting on her box beside Mrs. Marie-Claude Couty, is extremely sure of herself, despite her youth; as for Fenouille de la Vallée des Troglodytes, sitting facing Mrs. Claude Courprie, she has all of the impassiveness of a champion used to being acclaimed in numerous dog shows, even though she is only two years old.

POLISH LOWLAND (OR NIZINNY) SHEEPDOG

It was only when the new classification by the World Canine Organization was adopted in 1990 that this name was given to the Polish shepherd, which used to be called the valley shepherd. As for dog-breeders, they use the term "Nizinny."

Like most European sheepdogs, part of its ancestry is to be found in primitive Asian sheepdogs. Its head is covered with bushy hair on the forehead, cheeks and chin. Measuring 20 inches, its body is longer than it is tall, with a flat, highly muscular back and oblique rear quarters. Its fur is long, thick and dense. It can be any color.

Eliaska and Comte, known as Droopy Z Doliny, who belong respectively to Miss Patricia Noël and Mrs. Christa Lochner, are incapable of resisting the attraction of a tennis ball, especially when thrown by children, their favorite playmates.

PULI

The ancestors of this Hungarian dog, with an maximum height of 18 inches, were the primitive Asian dogs that accompanied nomads on their travels. It probably arrived in Hungary with the Magyars at the end of the ninth century.

It is solid, lean and very muscular. Its body, which forms almost an exact square, is entirely covered by long shaggy fur, which is uniform in color and wavy. It tends to become matted so that, when young, it can look like a Komondor. Its coat can be plain black, a reddish black, gray or white.

Bundas de la Bacska and Deresreti Kope belong to Mrs. Chagnard (above). Szegvarréti-Al-Palis, aged eleven, adores music like his mas-

ter Mr. Imre Horvath. He has a wide musical taste. He enjoys listening to the overture of Carmina Burana so much that he gives off a song-like bark (right).

Dutch sheepdog

It measures no more than 25 inches tall, and has a morphology similar to the Belgian shepherd. Not a surprising fact since it is the product of crossing local Dutch dogs and Malinoises.

Its head is of average length and topped with straight ears. Its body is powerful and its back short, straight and strong.

The first specimens of this breed appeared in France in the 1980s. Eros du Domaine des Crocs Sanglants, who belongs to Miss Sophia Anastassiades, has made a good start as a guard dog. He belongs to a common short-haired variety. Although the coat is wiry, it is not too short and can be brown, yellow or ginger brindled with gold or silver.

There are two other varieties:
• a wirehaired coat which is rather harsh to the touch, with few or no wavy hairs;
• or a third one, with long, flat and harsh fur.

BERGAMO HERDER

This breed descends from Asian mastiffs crossed with local dogs from the province of Bergamo, in northern Italy.

As is shown by Usmina dell'Albera, who belongs to Maria Andreoli, this middle-sized sheepdog's upper body is covered by abundant, extremely long hair, which is resistant and coarse, while on the lower body it forms long hanging tresses. This gives it a similar look to Hungary's Komondors and Pulis.

Its coat is generally gray, but can also have patches of all shades between gray and black. More rarely, it can also be black with a scattering of white patches.

It is rustic, robust and well proportioned.

PYRENEAN SHEEPDOG

This French breed certainly descends from the Tibetan terrier, whose descendants accompanied the Suevians when they invaded Gaul under Ariovista. Established in the high valleys of the Pyrenees in Bigorre, they remained there until the end of the nineteenth century, which helped them remain pure. There are two varieties with the same morphological characteristics.

The "longhaired" variety has abundant fur, which is "brushed up" on its cheeks and the sides of its snout. Mrs. Claudine Brault's Torquade de l'Estaube (right) is an excellent example.

For the "smooth-face" variety, see page 37.

The body is quite lean, the back short and the hindquarters oblique. The coat can be fawn, as is the case with Torquade de l'Estaube, gray or harlequin.

Its lively features and great vivacity of movement give it a highly characteristic appearance. Given its rather pugnacious nature, it needs a firm yet skillful master. It is a rural dog that needs plenty of exercise.

SHETLAND SHEEPDOG

The Shetland Isles, to the north of Scotland, contain numerous flocks of sheep. To guard them, the shepherds imported collies from the mainland and Nordic dogs from Iceland. Crossing them resulted in the Shetland.

At 15 inches, this sheepdog looks like a miniature collie. Its form is harmonious, with a long head topped with small ears, a muscular neck and a long body with a straight back. As a working dog, it can tolerate bad weather and has beautiful fur consisting of long, straight, stiff hair. It can be fawn flecked with black, black with fawn markings, or a blue with black markings. There can be some white on its chest, throat, limbs or the tip of its tail, except if the coat is black and tan, in which case there is not the slightest trace of white. Its coat can also be black and white—which is extremely rare in France—like that of Eustache who, alongside Blissful's Herlin and Guerlain Blue de Romanière, are putting up a watchful guard in front of Mrs. Catherine Lecomte.

PYRENEAN SHEEPDOG

Florac du Val Soannan and First du Val Soannan, who sit on either side of David Reilhac, perfectly illustrate the specific characteristics of the smooth-faced variety: they are slightly larger, their heads are covered with fine short hair, they have a slightly longer snout.

AUSTRALIAN CATTLE DOG

This breed was created in the second half of the nineteenth century by Australian breeders who wanted a dog capable of leading flocks over the immense territories they had to cover. A result of crossing dingos (tamed by the Aborigines) with European sheepdogs, this is a strong, compact working dog, full of stamina and extraordinary power. Its head is topped with upright slightly pointed ears. Its body is longer than it is tall—it measures a maximum 20 inches—with a strong horizontal back. Its smooth, wiry fur, which lies flat, is well suited to protecting it against bad weather conditions.

Its coat is either blue, like Gribouille de la Bakia, sometimes with black, blue or tan patches on the head, or a speckled red with occasionally dark red markings on the head. Gribouille never deserts Miss Laurence Courtin, who greatly appreciates her tenderness and cleverness.

BEARDED COLLIE

Its name describes it. Its ancestors were the Roman sheepdogs that arrived in Britain with Caesar's legions. Its fur often leads beginners to mistake it for an Old English sheepdog, even through the latter is stronger and has a shortened tail, while the Bearded collie's tail reaches the bend of its knees.

Of an average size—22 inches at most—it is quite long and despite its solid build not very heavy. The hair on the dog's head becomes longer as it reaches the chest, thus forming the characteristic beard which gave it its name. Its straight, wiry, abundant fur must never be brushed. Its coat can be different colors: black, gray, brown, blue or beige with or without white markings.

The Bearded collie has a working dog's temperament: alert, curious, lively and active. It detests solitude. It is extremely sporty, merry and frisky. While Clovis du Kastell a Labous Mor was training the day before an agility competition, he jumped so high that he hit Mrs. Françoise Pouliquen in the face, giving her a splendid black eye.

SAARLOOS WOLFDOG

In about 1920, a Dutch dog-lover called Saarloos decided to create a new breed of sheepdog by crossing a she-wolf and an Alsatian. Aware of the considerable difficulties he would face, he consulted some geneticists. After his work had been interrupted by World War II, he started again in the 1950s. He died before completing his project. Fortunately, the Dutch national cynophile association took over, and the breed was recognized in 1975, when it was considered to be stable.

This large dog, which can measure as much as 30 inches, is longer than it is tall, powerful, and looks like a wolf. It has wiry,

straight hair, providing a coat that can vary between light and dark black, light to dark brown, or from light cream to white.

Mrs. Souquière, who first introduced the breed into France, says that for a Saarloos wolfhound to be as attached to its masters as Naima Belladonna de Louba-Tar is to hers, the master must be kind and extremely patient, given this breed's independent tendencies.

MAREMANER HERDER DOG

The distant ancestors of this breed were the Asian mastiffs that accompanied the Mongols to Europe in the middle of the thirteenth century. These mastiffs were then crossed with local dogs from the Abruzzi region (in central Italy) and from Maremma (by the Tyrrhenian Sea). It can reach 29 inches, is powerfully built and, with its rustic yet distinguished appearance, is a beautifully vigorous dog. Its head is like that of a white bear. Its body is covered with long, abundant coarse hair, sometimes slightly wavy, of a plain white color yet occasionally with a very small number of ivory, bright orange or lemon yellow markings. This athlete must not be confined in a small space.

Dandalo de la Vallée Macchia is absolutely uncompromising when he stands guard on Mr. Mario Massuci's property. On the other hand, he is very tolerant and extraordinarily patient with his master's children and the Yorkshire terrier which shares their games, since he even allows it to make off with his bone.

Welsh corgi

In Britain, this Welsh dog is considered to be the descendent of primitive dogs that arrived there with the Celts several centuries B.C. However, it seems rather to have been product of crosses between local Welsh dogs with the Visigoths' spitz (Västgötaspets) which went with the Vikings during their raids on the English coast during the eighth and ninth centuries.

Very short (12 inches), it has great vigor and stamina, is a hard worker and is always in action. Its head makes it look like a fox, and it has rather large ears. Its body is long and powerful. This breed has two varieties.

Welsh corgi (pembroke)

This breed has only a tiny stub of a tail, and its coat consists of average-length straight hair, which is never soft, wavy or very harsh. It was introduced to the Court of England by George V, and is the favorite dog of his daughter Queen Elizabeth II.

Pemland Music Masters, Venwoods Gambling Man and Blackbird de la Caverne des Anges are crazy about soccer. Anytime Mrs. Jocelyne Thomas takes them for a walk near a playground where soccer is played, they are eager to run to the players and try to join in.

Welsh corgi (Cardigan)

This dog's wiry short- or medium-length fur forms a coat that can be any color, with or without white streaks, provided white does not dominate. Its tail is of average length. Droupy of Saint Hilaire's Park, Dark Pearl of Saint-Hilaire's Park and Gareth of Saint-Hilaire's Park, who belong to Mrs. Maurice Boulon, have managed to convince the family cat to satisfy their cravings by slipping under the fence and pushing through it any nuts that have fallen to the ground.

Old English sheepdog

The name of this dog comes from the fact that it an extremely old breed, derived from Roman sheepdogs crossed with other dogs from the continent at the end of the seventeenth century. Many breeders have come up with other hypotheses, but all lovers of this breed agree that its ancestors were longhaired sheepdogs. Since its official name is rather long, the British have given it a nickname based on its physique—the bobtail.

Measuring 22 inches on average, it is a strong dog with a compact but well-proportioned appearance. It is covered with wiry hair, which is not straight but shaggy. Its coat is gray or blue, with or without white markings.

Stocky and muscular, Tottel Free Mason at Ebonyivory and her daughter Ivory's Georgia Brown, who pose quietly beside Mr. and Mrs. Claude Ritter, amble along like all bobtails when they are in action. They trot by simultaneously lifting and dropping the limbs on one side. The resulting sway is rather reminiscent of the gait of a bear.

PODHALE

This large Polish dog standing at 28 inches is the product of crosses between Polish mastiffs and dogs from the Carpathian mountains in the Tatras region on the border of Poland and Czechoslovakia. The fact that this region remained isolated until the end of the nineteenth century greatly contributed to the breed's purity, better known as the "sheepdog of the Tatras."

Its head, with a strong and relatively pointed snout, has rather thick medium-length triangular ears level with its eyes. With its long, bulky, compact body it gives off a strong impression of power and vitality. The fur on its head is short and dense, while the fur on its body is thick, long, harsh to the touch, straight or slightly wavy, creating a sturdy plain white coat.

There was an immediate attraction between Fully du Pic du Roc Blanc and Mr. Christian Cerf. When Mr. Cerf visited the breeder, Fully, then eight weeks old, immediately went toward him. They have been together now for sixteen months.

KUVASZ

Its great height—up to 30 inches—makes this Hungarian dog look both powerful and noble. Its long head is topped with high ears, which flop down next to the scalp. Its body is long, and its hindquarters somewhat drooping. Its tail, which points down to its knees, is straight as far as its tip.

Its coat consists of white, medium-length coarse hair, which is wavy and slightly stiff. Full of stamina, it can trot effortlessly for 15 to 20 miles.

Mrs. Elisabeth Agnoux brought Portam Öre Döllar from Hungary when he was just seven weeks old. He has adapted perfectly to his life in France.

KELPIE

This noble Australian sheepdog's solid muscular frame and flexible limbs give it enormous stamina. Mr. Patrick Lusso, a biologist in Nouméa, took advantage of a trip to France to exhibit Goofy du Domaine de Ouassio at several European dog shows, and especially at the one organized by the Central Canine Society in Paris. Goofy won top awards wherever he was exhibited.

This breed is the result of a cross between Scottish sheepdogs imported to Australia in 1870 and a local bitch, a descendent from the collies that had accompanied the first European settlers. This bitch was called Kelpie, and her name was given to the breed, which was officially recognized at the beginning of the twentieth century. The kelpie is between 18 and 20 inches tall, and its head is topped with straight medium-length pointed ears, rather like a fox. Its neck is strong, its hindquarters long and drooping. Its coat, consisting of a double set of hard, stiff hair, can be tan, red, red and tan, or chocolate and blue. Lively and enthusiastic, this remarkable sheepdog is docile and devoted.

BORDER COLLIE

This breed is the result of crosses made in the Middle Ages between various breeds of British sheepdogs, which themselves descended from Roman dogs. The word "border" in its name comes from the fact that sheep breeders in the borderlands between Scotland and England were so taken by its courage, stamina and sway over a flock that they adopted it as their favorite sheepdog.

Of modest height—about 21 inches—this rustic dog has a fine long head, a strong muscular neck, with a rather long body and powerful broad back. Its coat consists of dense hair of an average texture, which can be any color.

The transformation of this collie into a household pet has made it even more appreciated as a sheepdog, since it has lost none of its rural nature. In France, the Border Collie Association, which manages the technical running of the breed under the direction of the Central Canine Society, intends to maintain it only in its role of a working dog. Mr. Antoine Brimbœuf, a shepherd in Rambouillet, greatly appreciates Dan. This three-year-old border collie's help is essential to him when he takes his large flock on its daily maneuvers.

PINSCHERS AND SCHNAUZERS, MOLOSSIANS,

SWISS MOUNTAIN AND CATTLE DOGS

Although all dogs, even lap dogs, instinctively try to protect "their" territory by alerting their masters as soon as an intruder tries to force his way in, not all of them are suited to the job. A guard dog must, of course, sound the alarm when it detects something wrong, but it should do so only when really necessary. A good guard dog must combine a cool head with great vigilance, good judgement and an ability to dissuade the intruder. When necessary, a guard dog must incapacitate the intruder without hurting him or, at least, hold him down until its master is in control of the situation. Finally, it must have great physical prowess and stamina, qualities necessary to guard an isolated house and, even more so, a large property.

The dogs possessing these qualities have been assembled in the first section of the second group: the pinschers and the schnauzers.

For many years, flocks were decimated by various predators (wolves, bears, jackals, pumas, jaguars and lynxes). To protect them, shepherds used powerful dogs that lived permanently with their charges and had just one mission: to protect them from attack. Shepherds today don't fear such ferocious predators, but they have new threats, such as stray dogs. These are generally dogs that have been abandoned; they have returned to an almost wild state and live together in packs like wolves. Many flocks have fallen victim to such attacks, and shepherds are increasingly reintroducing protection dogs in their flocks.

Such use remains relatively limited, however, and flock protection dogs are most often used as guard dogs, like those in the first section. Yet their particular morphology justifies the creation of a second section in the second group, the "Molossians." These dogs have powerful snouts, drooping ears, bulky heads and bodies, a thick skin that is sometimes loose, and are rather tall.

This is not surprising because to oversimplify, they all have a common ancestor—a primitive Asian mastiff. After the last floods of the Quaternary era, the falling water level encouraged Tibetan tribes to leave their high plateaus along with their primitive mastiffs and gradually to travel as far as the Middle East. Tibetan mastiffs were thus the forefathers of the large Assyrian mastiffs that were so highly reputed in days gone by. Later, other migrants left Assyria with their mastiffs and headed for the Mediterranean. They colonized Greece and Italy, then gradually moved into the Balkans, Germany, the Iberian peninsula, Scandinavia and the British Isles. Such waves of migration also moved in the opposite direction. Nomads from Tibet moved into Southeast Asia, across China and then, having crossed the Bering Straits, filtered down into the interior of North America. Thus, after crossings with local dogs, the primitive Asian mastiffs are the forefathers of all of the breeds in the subgroup "Molossians."

Finally, although Swiss cattle dogs all have mountain dog characteristics and can protect flocks, they can also lead and watch them, just like sheepdogs.

PINSCHER

The ancestor of this German dog was the famous dog of the Neolithic peat bogs, which became the companion of hunters and fishermen living on the North Sea coast. As the centuries passed, the descendants of this dog divided into two branches, which are differentiated only by the nature of their fur; the pinschers descend from the shorthaired variety.

Of average height, it has a robust head tipped with vertical ears, a square body and a highly-placed docked tail. Its short thick shiny fur forms a coat that can be either uniform (from brown to fawn) or else of two colors (black with red or brown markings). Etex de la Calellière, who belongs to Mr. Gaudfroy, amply displays the elegance of these lively, energetic dogs, which are not great barkers.

There is also a variety of miniature Pinscher, which is different for its size (10 to 12 inches instead of 17 to 19 inches on average) and by an additional coat color (brown or grayish blue with brown markings).

DOBERMAN

This breed was created in Germany and appeared in Apolda, near Erfurt in Thuringen, in the second half of the nineteenth century. It owes its existence to Frederick Ludwig Doberman, who created it by means of a series of empirical crossings, which he kept secret. From its morphology, it probably has pinscher blood, but the other elements remain unknown—pointer, mastiff, beauceron or greyhound? It doesn't really matter, for the result is what really counts.

The dobermann is rather tall, with a powerful muscular frame, a harmonious line and natural elegance heightened by its haughty demeanor and resolute expression. It is easy to understand why little Mylène Lecoq so admires the protection of Ertog Erphun von Rauberstolz.

The doberman's head is like a long sectioned cone. It is finely sculpted, and its ears are highly placed and erect. Its back is short and firm, and its legs extremely straight. Its short thick rough fur forms a shiny coat that is black and tan, chestnut brown and tan, or blue and tan.

It needs a master that is firm and fair, and who gives it enough exercise to satisfy its enormous energy.

AFFENPINSCHER

Despite its small size, this lively dog makes a good guard dog, adapting well to life in an apartment. It is part of the pinscher group because it, too, descends from the dogs of the peat bogs. The Germans named it because of its appearance, its abundant stiff fur, its vivacity and especially its apelike face ("Affenpinscher" means "monkey terrier").

As Diva de la Rochardière watches, Duck de la Rochardière poses in front of the white backdrop that Mrs. Dominique Laporte is holding to set off the purity of his black coat.

SCHNAUZER

Like the pinscher, its ancestors were the dogs of the peat bogs, but the schnauzer is part of the long-haired branch. This explains why, other than the difference of appearance due to their fur, there is a great similarity between these two German breeds.

The schnauzer is characterized by its beard and bushy eyebrows, which give it a quadrangular appearance, and its thick wiry fur. Its high energy level means that it needs plenty of daily exercise. There are three different-sized varieties. The two coat colors, black, and salt and pepper, can be found in the three varieties; the miniature schnauzers have two extra coat colors, black and silver, which is greatly valued, and white, which despite its rarity is considered to be a minor factor.

STANDARD SCHNAUZER

This dog stands between 18 and 20 inches tall, which means it can comfortably live in an apartment. Above left, Hweeko Rivale-Tiffany, who belongs to Mrs. Dominique Schall-Marx; above right, Mrs. Jeannette Seltz's Mihan Finland Prinsess is the first Finnish Schnauzer to be imported into France.

MINIATURE SCHNAUZER

Between 12 and 14 inches tall, this constantly alert dog is good at giving warnings. Mr. and Mrs. Peeters' Dylan de la Croix de Vilpert is a musician. When their granddaughter plays the flute, he "sings" by barking in time (right). Coralia Silvert de Furioso bravely defended her masters by attacking a large mastiff and causing it to run away (following double page). Mrs. Jeannine Roux-Capelli's Nimrod Bar-Lux (opposite).

GIANT SCHNAUZER

Measuring from 24 to 28 inches, rustic, powerful, fast and full of stamina, this is an ideal dog for protecting large properties. Clyde de Bujol (above), here watching over Julien Klimczak, possesses a keen sense of smell that allows him to detect deer and follow their trail with great precision.

Brahms de Monlaur has great sympathy for small animals. While Mr. Laurent Rabaté was having lunch, a yapping Brahms arrived, then pulled him over two hundred yards to help a small cat that was lying wounded in a cornfield (right).

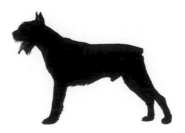

BULLDOG

A descendant of the mastiff, the British bulldog was one of the stars of the old-time dogfights. When these were outlawed, interest in this breed declined. It was saved by British breeders who worked on producing a dog that was lighter but still as bulky. The modern breed of bulldog was established at the end of the nineteenth century.

It has an extremely short face and a broad snub nose. Its limbs are athletic and its body well made. Its coat consists of short, thick, smooth fur that is either uniform red, "sooty" (uniform with a black mask or snout) or a mixture of white and red.

This dog has a delightful temperament belied by its severe appearance. Crazy Horse de Wounded Knee and Boo's Apple Cider love playing with the garbage can lid, which they vigorously drag around Mrs. Céline Bottussi's garden.

BULLMASTIFF

Are Mr. Jean-Pierre Guillemet and Edouard de Molossie sticking their tongues out at possible poachers? Definitely, for they know that poachers were responsible for the creation of the bullmastiff. During the second half of the nineteenth century, important British landlords became alarmed by the huge amounts of game that was being poached. So they asked dog breeders to create a dog that could trap poachers and hold them down until the gamekeeper arrived. This was successfully done by crossing mastiffs and British bulldogs, hence the name of the breed. Its skull is large and square, its head high with a short snout. Its V-shaped ears are highly placed and wide apart. Its chest is broad and high, its back short and straight. Its hind legs are powerful and straight, while its front legs are strong and muscular. It is well protected against the weather by its short wiry fur, which can be any shade of brindled fawn or red. Standing from 25 to 27 inches tall, it weighs between 110 and 130 pounds. It is solid, active, hard-working, faithful, strong and vigilant.

BOXER

The distant ancestors of this breed are the mastiffs that were used as dogs of war. But this German breed came into being in 1890 after a German breed, the "Bullenbeisser" (bull biter), which has now disappeared, was crossed with a British bulldog.

Measuring on average 24 inches and weighing in at about 65 pounds, this great athlete has a short black snout, vertical pointed ears and a muscular body. Its short shiny fur makes for a coat that is either uniformly fawn or has darker stripes. The boxer has the supple gait of a well-trained athlete. It needs plenty of exercise. Because of its enthusiasm, impetuousness and speed, it must be kept on a leash when taken for walks.

Following double page: *"Quo non ascender?"* Patrick Marizy seems to be thinking as he contemplates Clovis des Plaines du Nord. Fouquet's proud motto in fact perfectly fits this mascot for the advertisements of Kleber-Colombes tires.

GREAT DANE

When the Alani invaded Europe at the end of the second century, they came with impressive mastiffs that were used as dogs of war, and continued to be used as such until the Middle Ages. Later, these powerful mastiffs were crossed with Irish greyhounds, and the Great Dane was born.

Mr. Yves-Marie Merat's Droopy de la Templerie shows that, despite its large size—it stands at over 32 inches—the robust Great Dane is very well proportioned (see following double page).

Ephèbe des Terres de la Rairie, who belongs to Mrs. Vaslin-Soron, has the long expressive head that is so characteristic of great Danes— pendulous chops, a snout finishing vertically and ears cut into a point (right).

A firm yet gentle upbringing brings out the Great Dane's inborn good nature. Thus Colt des Fauvelles plays with the rabbits raised by Mr. and Mrs. Berson. Not only does he take their young for walks by holding them delicately in his mouth, but he does not hesitate to slip inside a hutch to warm them up if he thinks that the parents or young are cold.

NEAPOLITAN MASTIFF

This is Italy's national guard dog. It descends from Assyrian mastiffs introduced to Italy by the Phoenicians. The Romans used it as a dog of war, and also turned it into one of their circus stars.

Its head is large and short, covered with folds, its jaws well developed and its ears short and triangular. Its skin forms dewlaps in its neck. Its front and back legs are straight and its hindquarters oblique. The fur is short, dense, thin and smooth. The coat can be black, gray, mahogany or fawn. Wherever and whenever he goes out, Mr. Patrick Salomon

knows that he is in no danger while he is with Arno de la Fouinerie, whose fierce looks and imposing size are extremely dissuasive.

SHAR PEI

This breed descends from now-extinct Chinese mastiffs. The provinces of Kuang-si and Kuang-tong, by the south China Sea, were the cradle of this breed. It nearly disappeared when Mao Tse Tung decided to eliminate all dogs because they deprived people of food. Fortunately, some mainland Chinese took refuge in Taiwan in 1949 with their dogs. Then, during a study tour to Tai-lai, some American breeders discovered the Shar Pei, decided to save the breed and with that in mind acquired several males, which they took back to America.

While presenting Gabin des Roses de Porcelaine, Mrs. Cécile Aleman emphasizes a few typical characteristics of this breed: the many fine wrinkles that cover its forehead and cheeks, forming long folds, the small thick triangular ears, the folds covering the body, and the thick tail that is round at its base and finishes in a point. It is a pity that he is not showing his bluish-black tongue.

Standing 16 to 20 inches tall, it has very short bristly fur, harsh to the touch, and a black, tan, dark brown, beige or cream coat. Despite its sad appearance, it is in fact a good-natured dog. It used to be the great star of dogfights in China. Right: Mrs. Simone Bernier's Dollar.

BORDEAUX MASTIFF

Mr. Michel Guignard's Eros de l'Etang de Mirloup displays the typical head of a Bordeaux mastiff—low, large, trapezoidal and furrowed with wrinkles—as well as the bull-like neck.

The Bordeaux mastiff descends from the mastiffs that the Alani left in southwest Gaul when the Huns pushed them into Spain. When crossed with other local dogs, these mastiffs created the Aquitaine mastiff that later, during the nineteenth century, became France's national dog under its present name. The losses that breeders experienced during the two world wars were so great that the breed almost disappeared. It was saved by the determination of the breeders who, led by Professor Triquet, adopted rigorous but efficient methods of selection.

The Bordeaux mastiff is a thick-set, muscular colossus. His coat, made up of fine short soft fur, is plain mahogany or fawn.

MASTIFF

Like all mastiffs, the affection that Dogessa du Domaine du Cataou, who belongs to Mrs. Michelle Premat, shows her masters is as great as her weight.

The modern mastiff is the descendant of the great mastiffs that accompanied the Celts when they colonized Britain, several centuries before Christ.

This dog, which is England's national mastiff, is large, powerful and impressive, yet also well proportioned and well built. Its skull is long and wide, with a snub snout, a very broad lower jaw, a high large chest and an extremely muscular back. Its fur is short, flat against the body and fawn-colored.

DOGO ARGENTINO

The ancestors of Elton du Chêne le Gué, presented by Mr. Roberto di Blasi, were the dogs of war that accompanied Diaz de Solis when he landed near the Rio de la Plata. The descendants of these mastiffs were highly prized for dogfights. To make them even more ferocious, they were crossed with Corbova mastiffs, a breed that is now extinct. They soon became uncontrollably aggressive. Then, at the beginning of the twentieth century, Mr. Antonio Nores Martinez decided to create a breed capable of hunting wild boars, which caused great damage to his crops, and pumas, which massacred his livestock. To achieve this, he crossed the highly ferocious local mastiffs with Great Danes, pointers and Irish greyhounds, and managed to establish the modern Dogo Argentino in 1930.

Though less elegant and smaller, this dog is reminiscent of the Great Dane. It has short-cropped ears, a thick neck and extremely muscular limbs. Its coat consists of rather coarse, short hairs and is uniformly white. It has a well-balanced personality.

ROTTWEILER

This breed is the result of crosses between mastiffs used as dogs of war by the Roman legions, and dogs from the region around Rottweil, a town near Stuttgart, where the Romans had set up a base camp during their conquest of Germania. Exy du Trou du Diable, who belongs to Mr. Gilles Garnier, is a good example of the breed, with a medium build and a compact, vigorous stature. Her rusticity is combined with harmonious lines.

The head, of medium length, is topped with dangling ears that hang toward the front. The neck is firm and powerful, the rib cage large and the hindquarters broad. The legs are straight and widely placed. The black and tan coat consists of average length fur, which is harsh to the touch, dense and smooth. The Rottweiler trots along vigorously taking long strides.

FILA BRASILEIRO

When Alvares Cabral's comrades landed in Brazil in 1500, they were accompanied by Portuguese mastiffs. In the seventeenth century, the planters used their descendants to hunt down runaway slaves. Crossed with indigenous dogs, these mastiffs produced the Fila Brasileiro, which turned out to be very good at protecting flocks against jaguars. It has now become Brazil's police dog.

Standing between 26 and 30 inches tall and weighing at least 110 pounds, it has a robust frame, longer than it is tall, with a thick hide and a tail finishing in a point. Although the coat may be of any color, brindled fawn is the most common.

Kama amazes Mrs. Marie-Pierre Fournier with his dexterity. He opens the garden door, then closes it behind himself when wants to come inside. When he is thirsty, he goes to the bathroom and manages to turn on the tap in the bidet all by himself.

ATLAS SHEEPDOG

The precise origin of this Morrocan dog is still unknown, but it is certain that it comes from the upper Atlas Mountains, where shepherds used it to protect their flocks against jackals.

This rustic dog is remarkably powerful and mobile. Its head makes it look like a bear, while its back gives it a slightly plunging profile. Its hind legs are straight with muscular thighs, and its tail is long and bushy. The coat consists of very thick hair, about 2 inches long, which is good protection from both heat and cold. It is fawn, sandy, white and fawn, white and black, or tricolored. Dr. Id Sidi Yahia is justly proud to present Jaoui, who belongs to Mr. Ben Youssef. Jaoui has the strength and vivacity of his breed, as well as its extraordinary obedience.

CAUSACIAN SHEEPDOG

Originally from the mountainous region that extends from the Black Sea to the Caspian Sea, this powerful Russian dog stands 26 inches tall. Thanks to the inaccessibility of the valleys of the Caucasus, the breed has remained extremely pure. It is strong, weighs about 110 pounds, and has beautiful fur—which can be of any length.

This calm dog has a highly developed protective instinct. Hypteck, for example, found it strange that electricians were walking back and forth in front of Mr. and Mrs. Olivier's house. He leapt over the fence and forced them to climb up some telephone poles, where they remained until Mr. Olivier returned.

TIBETAN MASTIFF

The largest population of this breed can now be found in Nepal. The history of this dog parallels that of the tribes living in the mountains of Tibet. As well as protecting herds of yaks, it also guarded colonies of llamas.

Despite its respectable size, the modern Tibetan mastiff is smaller than the original mastiff, which is the ancestor of all of the Molossians. Its large noble head is topped with small dangling ears. Its shoulders and neck are covered with long, wiry fur, with a thick under-fur forming a mane. Its coat can be black, black and tan, gray, gray and tan or fawn. It stands at a minimum of 26 inches and has a supple gait and a tail that curls over its back.

Djouley de la Tour Chandos is a descendant of the first Tibetan mastiff to be imported into France. Mr. Jacques Thomas is still amazed to see him sleep on his back with his paws in the air.

ANATOLIAN SHEPHERD

In ancient times, this dog was used to protect flocks of sheep on the Anatolian plateau, bordered to the north by the Pontic Mountains, and to the south by the Taurus Mountains.

Standing from 30 to 32 inches tall, with a powerful frame, it can accelerate extremely quickly. Its characteristic features are its broad powerful head, thick muscular neck, solid legs and curved upper line. Its fur can be short or medium and any color, but is always dense. It tolerates all kinds of weather and is accustomed to living outdoors year round.

Ardent and dynamic, it is also extraordinarily patient with children, like A'Palah with the children of Mr. and Mrs. Cerda.

LANDSEER
Continental European type

Originally, this dog was just a variety of Newfoundland. When the English animal painter Landseer (1802-1873) was commissioned to paint a member of the British Lifesaver's Society, he chose to depict him with a black and white Newfoundland, the better to set off his subject. The picture was a great success and made this variety of Newfoundland so popular that British dog-lovers made it into a separate breed—which is pure morphological heresy—and naturally named it after the painter that had made it so popular. Later, the British lost interest, and continental European breeders were left to continue, hence the subtitle "continental-European type." This harmoniously shaped dog, as can be seen with Ulof Lonstrup du Kiouf standing below Mr. and Mrs. Breton, has remained similar to the Newfoundland and shares its lifesaving instinct. The difference is in its extremely long, smooth, dense fur, mixed with a lower layer that is thinner than the Newfoundland's. This fur gives it a white coat with discontinuous black patches.

PYRENEAN MASTIFF

Certain traits of this tall, powerful Spanish dog show its relation to France's Pyrenean mountain dog. This is not surprising, for the ancestor of both breeds was a primitive Asian mastiff.

With a maximum height of 32 inches, it has a broad skull and large solid head, topped by medium-sized drooping ears, which are flat and triangular. Its body is stout, its back powerful and its hindquarters wide and firm. Its strong thick tail has abundant tufts of fur. Its coat consists of dense thick fur and is generally white with gray or yellow patches, but it can also be brown, black, gray, beige or yellow. This strong, courageous and quiet dog is also distinguished by extra-

ordinary tenderness to its masters. Xoxona de la Tajadera del Tio Roy, aged fifteen months, throws herself at Mr. Jean-François Trimolet's feet as soon as he sits down. And, whenever she can, she shows him her affection by giving him a good licking.

PYRENEAN MOUNTAIN DOG

This breed arrived in the high valleys of the Ariège a long time ago. It was one of the Counts of Foix's favorite dogs. Its large size should eliminate the occasional confusions between it and the Pyrenean shepherd.

Measuring up to 32 inches tall, it has a powerful build. Its large snout narrows at the tip. Its chest is wide and deep, back fairly long and hindquarters oblique. Its flat abundant fur is supple and quite long, making for a magnificent coat that is generally plain white, with a few light yellow patches, or a uniform wolf-gray.

Mrs. Françoise Vidal's Delfin d'Elissacilio displays the elegance of the Pyrenean mountain dog. It is easy to understand why its harmonious figure attracted television producers, who honored it in the fine French television series devoted to Gaston Phébus, Comte de Foix, and made it the heroine of the series "Belle et Sébastien," which has delighted generations of children.

BERNESE MOUNTAIN DOG

The origins of this breed are controversial. However, all dog-lovers agree that its ancestors were good working dogs as early as the Middle Ages. The mountain folk of the high valleys in the canton of Berne generally used it to deliver their milk to the local cheese-maker in pails on a cart, which the Bernese mountain dog dragged along winding, bumpy paths.

Fusain, Romain Paty's confidant, is a good example of this fairly large utilitarian dog (26 to 28 inches). The Bernese mountain dog has a powerful head, muscular neck, broad chest, straight back and rounded hindquarters. Its coat is black with reddish brown patches on its cheeks and legs. Its chest is white. Its fine fur is smooth, long and slightly wavy.

TERRIERS

Dr. Fernand Méry was not only a great and popular animal lover, he was also an eminent cynologist who wrote numerous works concerning the origins and evolution of the canine species. He thus revealed the appearance in Egypt during the Middle Empire (2100 to 1850 B.C.) of a small, rather elongated dog that looked like a basset hound. Had it derived from an Egyptian greyhound? Fernand Méry remained silent on this point. He simply stated that he had discovered no earlier documents referring to this dog. Since the Phoenicians had already colonized the Syrian-Palestinian coastline in the second millennium B.C., and were thus neighbors of the Egyptians, it is possible that the descendants of this dog had evolved in Phoenicia and that Phoenician sailors took some of them with them during their voyages to the British Isles. This hypothesis is accepted by numerous cynologists.

Whatever the real story, it is certain that short-legged dogs, capable of pursuing badgers and foxes into their dens, thrived in the British Isles more than 2,000 years ago. And in fact, most of the modern breeds of terrier come from Britain.

The creators of these breeds tried above all to obtain dogs that could hunt foxes, badgers, martens and polecats underground, and destroy rodents. This is why these breeds are generally rather aggressive, dynamic and courageous. They also share many morphological characteristics, such as their small size, which enables them to crawl into burrows, and their powerful jaws.

With the arrival of modern methods of pest control, terriers have been used less and less to carry out their initial task. Only three breeds are officially still used (the fox terrier, the German hunting terrier and the airedale, although the latter hunts only above ground). The other breeds are generally pets, and it is rare that their masters make them work.

KERRY BLUE TERRIER

At about 20 inches, this is the largest of the Irish terriers. Created in the nineteenth century, it probably resulted from a cross between various terriers from the county of Kerry. Its powerful head is crowned with thin ears near the front. The body is muscular and well developed. Its broad back is straight, and its thin tail is erect. Its smooth, abundant, wavy fur can be any shade of blue. Mr. and Mrs. Rochette rightly claim that if the Kerry blue does use its strength to gain other dogs' respect, it can also be sociable.

Hazel-Boy Grenemore is an excellent example of this trait.

BEDLINGTON

This breed was obtained by crossing a Dandie Dinmont terrier with a whippet in Northumberland. The miners of the region appreciated its remarkable qualities as a ratter and, at the beginning of the nineteenth century, used it to destroy the rodents that plagued their mineshafts.

Of average height, it measures about 16 inches. This is a gracious, supple and muscular dog. Its pear-shaped head, long neck and arched back make it look like a lamb, even more so given that its thick fur tends to curl. Its coat is blue, fawn or brown.

The Bedlington is generally as friendly to its masters as Wetop Juggler is to Mrs. Mallet. While constantly trying to prove its loyalty, it has still not lost its original vivacity and liveliness.

LAKELAND TERRIER

This Scottish terrier originated in the nineteenth century, in the lake district by the western border of Scotland, near the Irish Sea. Like the Border terrier, which comes from the same region but to the east, its job was to kill the foxes that were decimating the flocks of sheep.

Elegant, with a well proportioned head, its ears are V-shaped. Its back is short and strong, its tail docked and erect. Its maximum height is 15 inches, and its fur is dense and wiry. Its coat can be black and tan, blue and tan, red, blond, brown, blue or black.

Like Patterdale Ivory in Mrs. Liselotte Accarie's arms, Lakeland terriers make perfect pets. But they still have not lost their hunting instincts.

Irish Glen of Imall terrier

Although rare, this Irish dog belongs to one of the oldest breeds of terrier.

At 13 inches tall, its broad head is decked with slightly rose-shaped ears. It has a strong chest, an elongated body and a docked tail. Its fur is of medium length, coarse and either brindled blue or blond.

It was a formidable hunter, but is now generally a pet, as can be seen with Ivanhoe's Amadeus, pictured here with the daughter of his owner, Mr. Gerhard Knieling.

Irish terrier

Some cynologists consider that this breed already existed in the eighteenth century. In fact, it does not seem to have been created until the late nineteenth century, using various local breeds.

Its long head, with powerful jaws, is topped with small ears that droop down onto its cheeks. Its neck is long, its back extremely straight and its docked tail highly placed. Its wiry fur gives it a uniform red coat.

Fiery, impetuous and courageous, it has a good nature and, when at rest, it looks as calm as Joe von der Leimkaul, pictured here pressing himself against Jean-Paul Péresse. Joe's sociability does not stop him from showing his courage when necessary. After ousting eight boars from their wallow with his companion, he confronted a 360-pound sow to save a wounded dog.

FOX TERRIER

Between the fifteenth and eighteenth centuries, many authors wrote of the exploits of the Fox terrier. These accounts refer to two English breeds that are now extinct, the Black and Tan terrier, and the White terrier. The modern Fox terrier came into being in the nineteenth century from a cross between these two breeds, first the smooth variety, then, a few years later, the wire variety. The latter has become famous thanks to Hergé's comic books about the adventures of Tintin and his wirehaired terrier, Milou.

The Fox terrier has extremely powerful jaws, small V-shaped ears that droop down over its cheeks, a short straight back and a highly placed docked tail. Its coat is white with brown and black patches. Both varieties display great vivacity and speed. The French managers of the breed often talk of the similarity between its shape and that of a racehorse capable of covering long distances. The Fox terrier still has an inclination to dig out prey, and its strength makes it an excellent retriever of small game.

FOX TERRIER (SMOOTH)

This dog's fur is smooth, straight, flat, dense and abundant.
Smooth Touch At Travella is extremely sharp and always alert. Highly sociable, he is happy only when he is with Mr. Patrice Legros, who in turn knows that he can rely on him (above).
Below, Mr. Denis Lobjois's Eymar de la Vallée sous terre.

FOX TERRIER (WIRE)

This terrier's "wire" fur is extremely stiff, never woolly or silky, thick or shaggy.
All Fox terriers are headstrong and brave, but also rather stubborn. Therefore they need a master who can control them and give them space and time to work off their energy every day. If this is the case, this dog will give its masters wonderful friendship and loyalty, as Farmer's Daky and Farmer's Flore give Mr. and Mrs. Ruano.

BLACK RUSSIAN TERRIER
Tchiorny Terrier

This breed was created after World War II according to instructions from Soviet authorities who wanted to provide their *kolkhozes* with dogs that could herd and defend flocks, as well as hunt.

Loyd Antoshka, standing above Mrs. Brigitte Monfort, shows the anomaly in classifying this large dog, which be 28 inches high, among the terriers. This comes from the fact that this breed has been recognized only very recently by the World Canine Organization which took the easy way out by classifying it according to its name. But it would be more logical to place it in the second group, for the giant schnauzer was almost certainly one of the breeds used to create it.

Strong and powerful, it has a long head with whiskers and a small beard, a high broad chest and a thick docked tail. Its coarse, wiry, abundant fur is extremely dense and forms a black coat that can contain gray hairs. Rustic and robust, it can adapt to any weather conditions.

PARSON JACK RUSSELL TERRIER

Jack Russell was studying theology at Oxford in the early nineteenth century when he became interested in fox hunting and terriers. He decided to create a breed of terrier corresponding to his hunting ideas. Unfortunately, after his death, the examples produced veered from the original type, and it was only in the 1970s that breeders returned to the model created by Parson Russell. This is why this breed is now only provisionally recognized by the World Canine Organization, which has imposed a probationary period, after which the Scientific Commission will check the conformity and homogeneity of the subjects that have been produced (French breeders have in fact already succeeded in reaching homogeneity).

Standing at 12 inches, with a finely balanced head, strong straight back and extremely solid legs, the Parson Jack Russell terrier is an active and swift dog, full of stamina and bred to work. Its thick coat is made up of coarse dense fur which can be either smooth or wiry. It is white and can contain fawn, lemon-yellow or black markings.

Gipsy du Pré Mil delights Mr. Bernard Lelyon. Not only has she won prizes in conformity and standard shows, but she also displays her innate abilities by triumphing in work trials in artificial burrows.

AUSTRALIAN TERRIER

When the first British settlers went to Australia, they took their dogs with them. The Australian terrier is the result of crosses made between various breeds of terrier that had thus been imported, particularly the Cairn terrier, the Dandie Dinmont, the Skye terrier and the Yorkshire terrier. The breed became firmly established at the end of the nineteenth century. Standing 10 inches tall, it is low and compact. It has a long head, with small pointed ears, a rather long body, a straight back and a docked tail. Its straight fur is of a wiry texture and gives it a blue or silver-gray coat, with tan patches on the legs and snout. It has kept its ability to hunt, but when necessary it can stay as calm as Dare Devil's

Magic Mirabunda. This terrier is a great athlete. Muffin, in Mrs. Bonne de Pracomtal's arms, started agility training at six months.

WELSH TERRIER

French dog experts affirm that the Welsh terrier descends from a terrier that lived with the Celts and took refuge with them in the mountains of Wales during the Roman invasion. For many centuries, it was used to hunt vermin, foxes, badgers and otters. It has thus become a great worker.

With a maximum height of 16 inches, it is slightly smaller than its ancestors. Its square build gives it a distinguished air. Its flat skull widens slightly between small V-shaped ears. Its back is short, its legs solid and its docked tail highly placed. Its wiry fur is extremely dense and abundant, giving it a black and tan or grayish black and tan coat, with tan head and legs.

An excellent working dog, full of vivacity, it can also be a great pet, as Athos des Chardons Saint-André is for Mrs. Reiter.

NORWICH TERRIER

This small terrier, which must be a maximum of 10 inches tall, was created in the late nineteenth century when a local tan-colored terrier (many varieties exist between Cambridge and Norwich), was crossed with Bedlingtons, Bull terriers and Irish terriers. Initially, there were two varieties: one with erect ears and one with drooping ears. Created by Mr Jones, they finally developed into two different breeds.

The Norwich terrier is solid, low and has a horizontal tail. Its snout is powerful and shaped rather like a wedge, and the medium-sized pointed ears must be erect—illustrated perfectly by Scarlet Runners Harlekin, nestled in Mrs. Bonne de

Pracomtal's arms. The fur is wiry, straight and lies flat against the body. The coat is red, blond, black and tan or grayish.

Harlekin is a courageous dog. One night, when the doorbell ran repeatedly, he sensed that his mistress was afraid and lay down over her to comfort her.

NORFOLK TERRIER

The only distinguishing characteristic of the Norfolk terrier is its ears. They are medium-sized, V-shaped, slightly rounded at the tip and droop forward over the cheeks. This essential difference is clearly visible in Miss Ardina Strüwer's Easy's That's Me, nicknamed Busy. Originally, the Norfolk and Norwich terriers were otters and rabbits hunters. Although they are now generally household pets, they

have retained their athletic abilities and, despite their short legs, are rapid runners. Busy often follows Miss Strüwer, who is a keen rider, and has no trouble keeping pace with her horse.

WEST HIGHLAND WHITE TERRIER

This breed owes its elegance to a mistake made by Colonel de Poltaloch. This great huntsman used to track foxes and rabbits with small fawn-colored Highland terriers. One day, thinking that he was firing at a fox hidden in the undergrowth, he killed one of his own dogs. He immediately decided that from that day forward he would have only white dogs and, after careful selections, managed to fix the West Highland white, known now to its many enthusiasts as the "Westie." It is often used in advertizing, which is understandable given its attractive appearance, elegance and mischievous looks, as in this group that consists of French Lover de Champernoune,

Call Me the Champ de Champeroune and Excentricity de Champeroune with Mrs. Amato and Mrs. Round-Vanlaer.

The Westie is compact and energetic. Its small, straight ears top its mischievous face. Its back is straight, its tail is short and erect and its straight, wiry fur is white.

SCOTTISH TERRIER

Scottish terriers, which descend from the Celts' terriers, have developed into different breeds according to regional selection criteria. In the northwest Highlands, they are squat with wiry fur. In the western Isles, they have elongated bodies and long fur. In the east, they have short legs and large heads. The Scottish terrier is, in some respects, a synthesis of various breeds of eastern terriers.

Its squat, powerful figure is well known to whisky lovers, as it can be seen on the label of a famous brand. It has a long head, topped with straight pointed ears, a muscular neck, a rather short back and a medium-length tail that can be erect or slightly curved. Its fur is

dense, wiry and coarse and forms a blond or brindled coat.

Although the Scottish terrier is no longer used as a working dog, it has still kept its ancestors' agility and energy. But, like Mrs. Delplanque's Emeraude des Rives du Morbras, it also has a distinctly dignified demeanor.

BULL TERRIER

This breed was created in about 1860 by Mr Hinks, a British dog-lover who always refused to reveal the breeds he had used. He is believed to have used the bulldog and the British white terrier with, perhaps, the greyhound and the pointer. The breed was fixed at the end of the nineteenth century. It became popular again with the American television series, "Hogan's Heroes," about the adventures of a fighter squadron that had a bull terrier as its mascot. There are two categories of this breed.

MINIATURE

This dog differs from the standard only in that its height is limited to 13 inches.
Erenden Macosqin of Aldringham, aged seventeen months (standing in front of Miss Fety), proves just how undeserved the bull terrier's bad reputation is. Thanks to a careful selection by French breeders, bull terriers produced in France are perfectly well-balanced.

STANDARD

This dog is characterized by its long, oval head, topped by small, slim straight ears. Its back is short and straight and its short horizontal tail is low. Its fur is flat, short and harsh to the touch, creating a coat that can be pure white or black, red, fawn or tricolored, provided white is the dominant color. Neither its height nor its weight is limited. What is important is that the dog be well proportioned.
First Sitting Bull du Mackcastel's behavior surprises Mr. Michel Gauvrit each evening: he slips into the living room, collects the cushions from the armchairs and carefully takes them to the corner of the house where he sleeps, making a comfortable bed for himself.

AMERICAN STAFFORDSHIRE TERRIER

This American breed is the result of crosses between the bull terrier and the Staffordshire bull terrier, established in England. The Americans, keen on dog fighting, were attracted to this breed and took several dogs to the United States, where they created an official breed.

To the left, Mr. Destrebecq's Energy du Parc de Combreux. With its high, medium-length head topped with short erect ears, high broad chest, muscular body, short slightly sloped back and short tail, it gives an impression of great power. It stands about 19 inches tall. Its fur is short, dense and harsh to the touch and shiny. Activity is essential to this energetic, dynamic breed. It can be an excellent guard dog when correctly trained, but its master must use firm discipline.

Miss Berruet points to Hagele's Hotshot, nicknamed Charly (belonging to Mr. Frédéric Chauvineau) as an example of a perfectly well-balanced dog, and regrets the fact that some people in the United States train the American Staffordshire to make it dangerous. This is a disservice to the dog, as the media perpetuates negative generalizations about this breed.

STAFFORDSHIRE BULL TERRIER

The dog was created by crossing the old bull terrier breed with various other British terriers in Staffordshire. This terrier became extremely popular in Britain after World War II. Measuring between 14 and 16 inches tall, it is well-proportioned and very muscular. Its head, topped with roseate, half-erect ears, is short and high. Its neck is short, body stocky and legs solid. Its coat is red, fawn, black, blue, variegated white or pure white. The fur is smooth, short and thick.

Intrepid and brave, it needs a firm but kind master. This lively dog will then be as calm and affectionate as Fox Lady de la Lune de Sang and Funny Droopy de la Lune de Sang are with Mr. and Mrs. Petit.

DACHSHUNDS

The fourth group is unique in that it contains just one breed. This classification was the subject of long debates in the World Canine Organization, as several countries objected to the idea of one breed constituting an entire group. But Germany, the breed's country of origin and thus its technical director, demonstrated that the dachshund's physical characteristics and skills make it a separate breed.

Although the World Canine Organization was not entirely convinced by Germany's morphological arguments, it did agree that this formidable working dog performs highly diverse tasks:
• It hunts foxes and badgers in burrows, like the terriers that form the third group.
• It hunts above ground by "voice tracking"; in other words, the dachshund barks and follows a rabbit's or hare's trail as do scent hounds in the sixth group. Furthermore, the dachshund often works in packs like scent hounds.
• It can follow large, wounded prey by tracking its blood. For many years, this was the only dog to do so, but it has since been joined by various breeds in the seventh group (pointers).

These arguments were sufficient to convince the World Canine Organization.

The exact origin of this German basset is still a controversial subject among cynologists. Some believe that it came from Egypt, but supporters of this hypothesis have not explained how it traveled from Egypt to Germany. Others think that it descended from German brachets—scent hounds—in the Middle Ages. This hypothesis seems the most plausible.

The dachshund has flat, medium-length, rounded ears. They are placed high and behind its long head. Its lean, muscular neck is quite long. Its body is long and compact.

Intelligent and lively, it barks only when necessary. When this working dog has a firm but fair master, it is an excellent companion.

There are three categories of dachshunds, distinguished by their fur: short, wiry and long. Each category is subdivided into three sizes:
• Standard: this dachshund weighs a maximum of 20 pounds, the ideal weight being between 14 to 16 pounds;
• Miniature: this dog must weigh under 9 pounds at eighteen months and the chest measurement may not exceed 14 inches;
• Rabbit (rabbit-hunting dachshund): this dog may not weigh more than 8 pounds at eighteen months, and the chest may not exceed 12 inches.

SMOOTH-HAIRED DACHSHUND

Short, thick, shiny flat fur covers its entire body.

MINIATURE SMOOTH-HAIRED DACHSHUND

Fergusalbert de l'Ancien Relais, a black and tan miniature Dachshund with Mr. Jean Wattement.

MINIATURE
SMOOTH-HAIRED DACHSHUND

With the exception of Bout'chou de la Voûte azurée, a standard Dachshund (to the right), Mrs. Jeannine Chopin presents a fine set of miniature smooth-haired dachshunds, in particular Douce and Patchouli de Sadiana (preceding double page).

LONGHAIRED DACHSHUND

This dog's fur is silky, soft, flat and slightly curly.

LONGHAIRED RABBIT
DACHSHUND

Frissondamour du Dom Teckel and Sébastien Jacops (above).

MINIATURE
LONGHAIRED DACHSHUND

Félicihossy and Elodie Jacops (right).

Standard longhaired dachshund

Five standard longhaired dachshunds surround Mrs. Gérard Goguelat, who particularly admires Fonzie de la Pannecière for her ability to climb trees when playing with Pénélope, the young cat of the house.

Wirehaired dachshund

This dog's fur is the same length all over the body and forms a dense, wiry coat.

Standard wirehaired dachshund

Mrs. Serge Agogue presents three standard wirehaired dachshunds. Yak Vom Frischhofsbach stands out from the group.

MINIATURE WIREHAIRED
DACHSHUND
Cyrano du Creux de la Sablière
and Mr. Ernest Roussel-Lagache.

WIREHAIRED RABBIT DACHSHUND

In front of Mr. and Mrs. Brunelli, Félix le Chat de Ker Ki Douar, a chocolate wirehaired rabbit dachshund, stands out against the three black and tan miniatures with him.

STANDARD SMOOTH-HAIRED DACHSCHUND

Fleurine de Mostavielle, perched on Mr. Serge Mallet's shoulder, displays two of the dachshund's characteristics: sociability and liveliness.

GREENLAND DOG

Originally from Greenland, this dog is full of strength and stamina and is used to working in the harshest conditions of the Arctic. It has successfully participated in numerous expeditions to both the North and South poles, notably those led by Paul-Emile Victor, who has popularized the breed in France. Despite its tendency to run away from home, the Greenland dog is sociable. However, it is exceptional for it to be as affectionate to its master as Amaraqs D'Giro is to Mr. Delente, for it is not naturally demonstrative. It stands at least 24 inches, has a strong neck, very broad chest, an extremely muscular body and a straight back. Its coat is made up of dense, straight, coarse fur, and can be any color.

Kept outside constantly by the Greenlanders, it has become strong and can easily withstand both cold and heat. It is now used as a sled dog only by the Eskimos and by Arctic hunters.

ALASKAN MALAMUTE

Stardom has not changed Umalooil Over Vale and Dale's character. Although he has been in numerous television commercials, a serial and the video clip for Julien Clerc's song "Fais-moi une place," he still remains extremely attached to Mrs. Michèle Raust de Palma. This attachment to its masters is one of the characteristics of this large powerful dog, originally from the Bay of Kotzbuhe on the Bering Straits. Its name comes from the Eskimo tribe to which it provided indispensable help for centuries. It is the largest of the sled dogs. With its deep compact chest and vigorous and powerful build, it carries out its work efficiently, pulling heavy loads over great distances.

Its eyes are brown, preferably dark brown, and never blue. Its thick, coarse coat has two color combinations (gray and brown, or black and white) or else is pure white. It adapts well to bad weather conditions but dislikes great heat.

Full of dignity, calm and determination, Umalooil Over Vale and Dale is inseparable from his mate, Arctic Black Gipsy Over Vale and Dale, who, under Mrs. Raust de Palma's direction, participates with him in the work trials organized by the French Nordic dog club.

SAMOYED

This large dog—an average 23 inches—takes its name from the Samoyeds, a tribe in northern Siberia. It kept their herds, hunted bears with them and pulled their sleds. Its ample, heavy, dense and supple fur forms a coat that can be white, or sandy and white. This energetic dog is robust and agile. Full of dignity, it makes an excellent pet that attaches itself to its masters, as can be seen with Mrs. Arlette Flamand when she talks of her relationship with Blue Sky's Dapper Dan and Ivory Madonna of Sameida (preceding pages).

NORWEGIAN ELKHOUND GREY

Standing at 21 inches, with an ample chest, a short and relatively compact body, this dog has a thick coat which is coarse and weather resistant and made up of long gray hair that is darker at its tips. Originally from Norway, it has always been considered a great hunter. Full of power, stamina and courage, it has a good nose, and for the Vikings it provided exceptional help in the difficult task of tracking elk.

In 1991, Central Canine Society finally accepted that its scent abilities could be evaluated in tests involving tracking the blood of large wounded game. The Forestry and Water Resource Commission are planning to use it to record popula-

tions of game animals in order to better protect them.

Despite its great sociability, the Norwegian elkhound is very independent. Although Djerva du Rocher de Sisyphe is very attached to Mr. and Mrs. Christian Collas, she decided to give birth to her first litter under their caravan, instead of in the specially prepared room. She then refused to feed them anywhere else.

FINNISH SPITZ

The ancestors of this breed were the companions of Finland's first inhabitants.

When looking at Finn' Fellow de la Cascade des Jarreaux in front of Mr. Robeaux, one might think that the Finnish spitz is a large dog, but this is an optical illusion caused by the camera angle. It is actually average in height—between 18 and 20 inches. Its body is almost square with a strong straight back. Its eyes, ear movements and wagging tail reveal its great vivacity and enthusiasm. Its short fur, lying close to its body, forms a ginger-brown or ginger-yellow coat. In Finland it is used for grouse hunting.

NORWEGIAN LUNDEHUND

This breed originally came from the Lofoten and Vesterälen Islands in the Atlantic, on the northwest coast of Norway. On the cliffs of these islands can be found many puffins, which the inhabitants of the archipelago capture live using these dogs. It climbs up the steepest cliffs with remarkable agility, for each of its feet is equipped with six claws, an exception in the canine species. Its coat, composed of rich dense fur, is ginger-brown, black or gray with white markings.

It is light and generally jovial and perky. Its extraordinary suppleness allows it to throw back its head onto its back. It then contracts the cartilage around its ears to make them watertight.

These two characteristics allow it to work in narrow damp caves, without letting water get in its ears. Attentive, discreet and friendly, Crow Hunter and Douchka have occasional outbreaks of atavism and use their climbing ability to clamber into henhouses, then carry the chicks out delicately in their mouths without hurting them, before placing them at Mrs. Robert's feet.

KARJALANKAR HUKOÏ RA

Karelia straddles the Russo-Finnish border. This extremely ancient breed comes from the Russian part of the region. After the 1917 Revolution, the Russians lost interest in this dog, and the Finns adopted it. It is of average height—22 to 24 inches—robust, strong and slightly longer than it is tall. It has a thick coat made up of stiff straight fur. It is black, preferably brownish or matte, with white markings or patches on its neck, chest, abdomen and legs. Its sense of smell is highly developed, which makes it of great help when hunting big game (bears and boar, which are abundant in Karelia), as do its perseverance and courage.

According to popular belief— which unfortunately is inaccurate here—this dog supposedly has a difficult character. Björnehusets Gaia always obeys young Chloé Meyer right away and is a loving, loyal dog.

ICELAND SHEPHERD

It is only natural that young Margot Lembrez be extremely proud to hold G'Käta in her arms, for it is the first Iceland sheepdog to be imported into France, thanks to Mrs. Jocelyne Thomas.

G'Käta belongs to a breed that has existed for one thousand years. In the tenth century, Iceland became home to a large number of Norwegian and Swedish immigrants. The immigrants' dogs naturally mated with the indigneous primitive spitzes, which are now extinct. The Iceland sheepdog derives from this melting pot.

Its coat consists of white wiry fur with fawn markings and black spots. This light, lively dog is an excellent flock leader. It can also be used as a guard dog. Made for living in the countryside, it becomes very attached to its masters and loves playing with children.

SWEDISH VALLHUND

The bright curious eyes of Hurtsfiels Halde and Drammerican's Biba, standing alertly in front of Miss Edwige Thomas, display their vigilance, ardor and energy, all typical characteristics of the Swedish vallhund. This small dog—13 inches—has adapted well to France, where the breed's first subject was imported by Mrs. Jocelyne Thomas in 1988.

It is an extremely ancient Swedish breed. The Vikings entrusted it with their herds and houses and took it with them in their longboats on their expeditions, particularly to the British Isles. This was how several of these dogs first arrived in Wales, where they mated with local dogs, creating the Welsh corgi, which greatly resembles it physically. Low to the ground, its elongated body is muscular and its neck long. Its wiry half-length fur forms a gray coat, with darker hairs on the back, the nape of the neck, shoulders and sides. It is a herd leader that can dominate any kind of cattle. Essentially a rural dog, it can adapt to city life.

SWEDISH REINDEER HERDER

Mrs. Catherine Agnus—seen here with her dogs Lumiturpa Baksu Bake (twenty months) and Katrin Onerva (four months), and Finntrix Tupu (three years) who belongs to Mr. Trichet—loves running by the sea with her four Nordic dogs. After taking part in the Nantes dog show, she took them to Saint-Brévin beach where they were so excited that they all fell into a deep pool of water. She was then able to see just how well they can swim.

The Finnish reindeer herder is a dog of average height—maximum 21 inches—slightly longer than it is tall. Its long thick coat is composed of stiff fur, which can be of any color. The first settlers in Iceland used it to guard their herds of rein-

deer. Very resistant, brave and easy to train, this rural dog makes an excellent sheepdog. It is also intelligent and calm, and is now generally kept as a pet.

GERMAN SPITZ

The ancestors of this dog lived with the first inhabitants of the lakeside towns. It fulfilled many roles: hunting, protection, sledding and companionship. Originally, the spitz was a large dog, but its morphology has evolved during the centuries, at first naturally, and over the last two centuries through selective breeding. There are five varieties of modern spitz, essentially distinguished by their size.

All spitzes have superb, abundant fur whose hair stands up above a dense under-layer. Their neck is covered with a large collar that forms a mane. Their fox-like head, bright intelligent eyes and the great mobility of their ears makes them look alert, curious and a little

mischievious. Their mistrust of strangers, faithfulness to their masters and attachment to their home adds to their excellent qualities as companions.

MEDUM-SIZE SPITZ

This dog measures from 12 to 14 inches. Its coat can be white, like Mrs. Jacqueline Peracini's Elphy du Périgord Vert, or black, brown, orange or wolf-gray. Queen Victoria had several of them, and enjoyed playing with them as relaxation from her heavy official duties.

Miniature spitz

This dog measures between 9 and 11 inches. Its coat can be orange—like Mrs. Monique Bourgalay's Elton du Bois de Moque Souris—or white, brown, black or wolf-gray.

WOLFSPITZ

This is the largest of the spitzes. On average it stands 20 inches tall. Fendy zum Asphof and Igmar vom Osterhof display the beauty of their black-speckled sandy coat. Their paws, thighs and tails are light and the rest of the coat is charcoal gray with light markings over the shoulders. Along with Fendy and Igmar, Mr. Benoît Wiart has five other Wolfspitzes. After the birth of his daughter, the seven spitzes took turns going to the baby's bedroom, where they stood vigilantly on guard in front of her crib.

MEDIUM-SIZE, MINIATURE AND POMERANIAN SPITZES

The medium-size, miniature and Pomeranian spitzes are often orange, like Dyleine des Lutins des Tilleuls, Elke du Val d'Almoyren and Eïka, who belong to Mrs. Véronique Le Bihan and Mr. Eric Fongarnan.

GREAT SPITZ

Standing between 16 and 20 inches, its coat can be black, brown or white, like Mr. Michel Bouleau's two great spitzes. He is particularly proud of Funky de l'Igloo des Edelweiss (the larger of the two).

POMERANIAN

This breed measures less than 9 inches. It can be wolf-gray, like Cassius du Val de l'Ange blanc, or orange like Voyou de l'Ange blanc, both of whom belong to Mrs. Jacqueline Desouche, but it can also be black or white.

HOKKAIDO

Mr. Takumi Ashibe, who lives in Paris, appreciates the presence of Kumatorow Kouri and Katsume Tomikawa Toyada, his two Hokkaidos. Faithful, obedient and affectionate, they contribute to the Japanese atmosphere in his home.

The Hokkaido lived with the Ainous in the Sakhalin, Kuril and Hokkaido islands to the north of Japan. In the eighth century, the Fujara clan seized power and pushed the Ainous back onto Hokkaido Island; this isolation helped conserve the purity of their dogs, which were generally used for bear hunting. It is now a guard dog. The Hokkaido, when in action, is swift, light and flexible. Of average height— 21 inches—and solidly built, it is well balanced. Its coat, composed of coarse straight fur, is black, ginger, brown or brindled.

AKITA

This large well-built dog is both stocky and well-proportioned. Originally from the province of Akita in Japan, it was the favorite companion of eighteenth-century Japanese nobles. In the nineteenth century, it was used in dogfights, before being replaced by the Tosa, a Molossian, and experiencing a rapid decline. After World War II, the Akita became popular once again. It is now Japan's national guard dog. Standing 27 inches tall, it has a harmonious build. Its coat, composed of coarse straight fur, is ginger, white or brindled.

Mr. Patrick Suard first encountered an Akita in 1979. He was sleeping on Chiba beach, near Tokyo on the Pacific coast, when he was awoken by a large dog which, though sitting on its hind legs, was staring at him and barking. Attracted by its bear-like head, slanting eyes and powerful yet elegant build, he obtained some information about the breed and purchased his first Akita. He has now been passionate about this breed for thirteen years, has started breeding them himself and praises their intelligence, docility, courage and nobility. It must be said that Daigorah and Kasuaga, standing on the podium, and Waka Obakosow and Hinaude Obakosow, in Mr. Suard's arms, justify his enthusiasm.

JAPANESE SPITZ

Even though, like all spitzes, its distant ancestor was the dog of the peat bogs, this is a relatively recent breed, the result of crosses between European and Japanese spitzes at the beginning of the twentieth century.

It is a small well-shaped dog—measuring about 12 inches—and well proportioned. Its coat, made up of straight, erect fur, is abundant and pure white. Its snout is pointed, its ears triangular and erect. It carries its bushy tail over its back.

The Japanese spitz is joyful, alert and brave. There are a few rare subjects in Europe, but none in France. Attracted by the international reputation of the Central Canine Society's annual dog show,

Signora Luisella Gecchinato came from Italy to display Midori, who received much attention and praise.

SHIBA

Originally from Hokurika, on the east coast of the island of Honshu to the northeast of Tokyo, this dog was previously used to hunt small game. It is now generally a pet.

It is a short dog—16 inches—but nevertheless well-proportioned and muscular, like Welshim Osanu at Vormund in Mrs. Catherine le Palec's arms. Its fur is coarse and straight. Its coat is black, black and tan, red, white or brindled. This lively, loyal and docile dog is both active and rapid. Like all of the "spitz type" dogs, it is extremely clean.

EURASIER

Diva du Font du Roy, Phébus de Parayraou and Freya de Parayraou are three of Mrs. Mattei's eight Eurasiers (preceding pages). This recent breed was created in the 1950s from crosses between the Wolfspitz and the Chow Chow. Of average height—21 to 24 inches—it is compact and well-built, with a coat composed of both short dense fur and medium-length fur. It is black, gray-black or fawn. Calm and open, it adapts to any living conditions and is notably faithful. It is vigilant but not noisy, and barks only when necessary.

IBEZAN WARREN HOUND

Introduced into Spain by Phoenician sailors, the remarkable qualities of this rabbit hunter led the Spanish to introduce it to the Balearic Islands, where rabbits were causing considerable damage.

The Ibezan Warren Hound is tall—up to 29 inches—and is a precocious hunter. Elodie (above) was only four months old when she caught her first rabbit. This attractive dog, with her red and white coat, is very attentive to the well-being of other animals. She took care of an unweaned kitten as well as she would have nurtured her own pup. She astonishes her owner Mr. Gilliot by the way she washes herself like a cat.

CHOW CHOW

The dog was the companion of the Huns, the Mongols and the Tartars, who used it as a guard dog and for hunting. The establishment of relations between the West and China, after the Franco-British expedition of 1860, allowed English breeders to become interested in this breed and start raising it. This is why the technical management of this Chinese breed is performed in Great Britain.

The Chow Chow stands between 18 and 22 inches, is compact, powerful, imposing and has dense abundant fur that can be long and brushed back, or short and straight. Its coat can be blue, like Oes—Ming—Chy—Nees, or a very light fawn like Arom—Pako, both of whom belong to Mr. Achille Lambert (right). It can also be whitish, or any shade of fawn.

Its lion-like appearance and grim expression, created by the wrinkles of the face, are characteristic. Other unusual aspects are its blue-black tongue and its short, stiff gait. It is dignified, calm and very attached to its masters despite an independent nature.

Pharaoh hound

This breed descends from a primitive African dog that accompanied Phoenician sailors during their expeditions. Some arrived in Malta, where they set up homes with their dogs. After taking possession of that island in 1800, the British became interested in the breed and christened it the "Pharaoh hound," because of its similarity to a greyhound that appears frequently on ancient Egyptian monuments.

The Pharaoh hound is of average height and has a well-proportioned body. Its short, smooth, shiny fur gives it a fawn coat with white markings.

It is a great rabbit hunter. In Esaü Gaillard du Croquet, who belongs to Mrs. Françoise Gaillard and is pictured presented by Mr. Herman, its noble poise is evident, as is its elegant carriage and erect ears. Its sense of hearing is extraordinary, and it hunts by ear as much as by sight.

Mrs. Gaillard has nicknamed Esaü "Gazelle" because of his speed and agility. Gazelle comes to see his masters each morning when they wake up, then impatiently waits for them to imitate the beating of a bird's wings with their hands, which he then pretends to hunt.

Cirneco dell'etna

Like the Pharaoh hound, the ancestor of this breed was the primitive African dog that accompanied Phoenician sailors. Some of these dogs settled in Sicily.

It is of average height, generally about 3 inches shorter than the Pharaoh hound. Its semi-smooth fur creates a "glassy" texture and gives a special appearance to its coat, which can be fawn and white or just fawn.

Mr. and Mrs. Henri Brelaud got Faetano in Italy when he was just three months old. He was born in Sicily, near Messina on the slopes of Mount Etna. Like all members of his breed, he is dynamic and extremely active. After two and half years of life together, his owners say that he is still as curious as on the first day and is both independent and very affectionate.

PORTUGUESE WARREN HOUND

The ancestor of this breed is a primitive African dog, introduced into the Canaries by the Phoenicians.

It is an extremely muscular dog with great intelligence and extraordinary vivacity. There are three varieties: large, 22 to 28 inches; medium, 16 to 22 inches; and small, 8 to 12 inches.

Elvira da Pria da Roberjo is the first dog of the small variety to be imported into France. The variety is so rare that Mrs. Jackie Bourdin had to wait two years before obtaining one. The fur is short, dense, smooth and fawn colored, but the Portuguese Warren Hound's coat can also be long, coarse and colored yellow, dark gray or faded black.

BASENJI

This dog's ancestors were already hunting with the Pygmies several thousands of years ago. It then became the companion of the Baschengi, a tribe based on the banks of the Congo in Western Africa. Later, the Egyptians considered it to be a sacred animal, responsible for leading the dead into the afterlife.

There are two varieties of Basenji, both of which have short silky fur covering their baggy skin:
•The "brush" type, which measures a little over 16 inches and has a light fawn coat with a large white breastplate.
• The "wood" type, which is somewhat smaller and thus better suited to equitorial life. Its coat is dark fawn, almost mahogany.

In Africa, the Basenji works as a tracking dog for Safari guides, while villagers use it as a guard dog. It is ideally a rural dog, as it tends to run away from home. It is very clean and does not bark.

SCENT HOUNDS
AND RELATED BREEDS

After this sixth canine category was formed, it was split into two subgroups: breeds used for hunting large game and other breeds used primarily for tracking wounded game.

When assigning distinct breeds to the first group, the Canine Organization based its decisions on the definition of a hound provided by Professor Triquet: "a hunting dog or hound with large, floppy ears that flushes out game thanks to a keen sense of smell and pursues it while continuously barking."

A hound must therefore possess a strong constitution, keen sense of smell, powerful bark and an ability to pursue game tirelessly. The hound should also be sufficiently familiar with the game it is meant to pursue, well versed in its habits and tactics while it is being chased, and familiar with the natural terrain in which the game normally thrives. To accomplish all of that, the hound must be adequately trained and bred for the right characteristics, that is, it must be specialized in the pursuit of a particular type of game.

Breeds that are specialized in the location of wounded game are assigned to the second group. This requires that the dog be able to pick up the wounded game's trail by detecting the blood spilled by the animal. The dog must be able to do this even when the trail has "gone cold," meaning several hours after the animal has left the vicinity.

Like other hunting dogs, bloodhounds must have a powerful bark, as this is the only means by which the hunter can follow the progress and direction of a high-speed chase through the countryside.

GREAT ANGLO-FRENCH TRICOLOR HOUND

English and French hunting parties do not use their dogs in the same way. In England, the dogs are essentially trained to hunt in the open. In France, on the other hand, they are let loose on the trail, whether hot or cold, to pursue it by scent while barking constantly to indicate the direction of the chase. Consequently, the dogs have different qualities to suit the different hunting styles. The English favor stamina and speed, while the French prefer a keen sense of smell and a superior bark. These qualities are obviously complementary, and so French hunters often cross the different breeds to find a balance of traits most suitable to the game of interest. Interbreeding in this manner has led to the creation of three hybrid Anglo-French subtypes, with each breed differing in color and size according to the different fea-

tures of the original strains. The large Anglo-French tricolor breed is the creation of a cross between the foxhound and the Poitevins. The form of the dog derives directly from the Poitevin. They stand 24 to 28 inches tall, with a fairly short snout and large head, flat ears of medium length, a large chest and a straight back. All these features attest to the sturdiness of the breed. The hair is short, more or less coarse and composed of three distinct colors, with either a black saddle or dispersed black spots. They are adept at working harsh terrain; they possess stamina and an excellent gait, a keen sense of smell and a pleasant, resounding bark. Specialized in hunting stag or deer, they are also easily adapted to hunting wild boar. The team from the Bonnelles hunting club is made up of large Anglo-French tricolors. Like all hunting

dogs, after a vigorous chase they enjoy a good rest together, nuzzling closely in a tightly-knit pack (following double page).
There are two other varieties of Anglo-French tricolors:
• black and white, whose frame recalls its Gascon Saintongeoise origins;
• black and orange, whose short snout and large head indicate its English origins.

FRENCH
TRICOLOR HOUND

This is the most recent of the French hunting dogs. It was originally bred by Mr. de Falandre during the middle of the twentieth century. The breed is the result of a cross between the large Anglo-French bi-

colors, whose Poitevin origins are evident, and Billys, a breed that is itself a mix of Poitevins and, quite possibly, the Blue Gascony hound. The breed was officially established in 1960.
This is a large, graceful and muscular dog. The dogs hunt as a team in orderly fashion. Its rather long head has ears that are somewhat large. It has a deep chest, a sloping back and a long, lifted tail. Its coat is short and soft and made up of three principal colors. A beautiful example of this breed is featured here accompanied by Mr. Benoît Dulac. This dog, a champion, is seven years old and belongs to the Normandie Piq'Hardi club.
The breed is used essentially to hunt deer, but can be adapted to hunt smaller game. There are also two other French breeds both used primarily for hunting deer as well.

BLOODHOUND

According to legend, this Belgian breed descends from dogs that Saint Hubert brought back to his abbey in the Ardennes after completing a mission in the south of France. Whatever the story, it is known that for centuries the monks raised large dog breeds to guard their remote monasteries. We don't know the precise origins of the particular breeds raised at the Abbey of Saint Hubert, but we do know that a breed of this name was maintained at the abbey. Records show that they were given as gifts to a number of French kings.

This breed is the origin of several other hunting breeds. The bloodhound was brought to England in the eleventh century, where it was rechristened because of its excellent sense of smell.

Judging from Ardent du Val Memorin, Dalton, Fallone and Djazz, who all belong to Mr. Creton, the bloodhound is a heavy, muscular, well-proportioned breed. It is an excellent tracking dog. The dog is usually used alone, but sometimes employed in small teams. The dog stands on average of 27 inches at the shoulder. It has a short, tight coat that is usually tan, black and tan or brown and tan in color. Its large head is typical: the skull is elevated and pointed, covered in a thick wrinkly hide with baggy jowls and long droopy lips. Its bark is powerful.

BILLY

This dog was created during the latter part of the eleventh century from a cross between the now non-existent French breeds—the Larye, Céris, Montemboeufs—and to a lesser extent, the Gascon Saintongeois. It is named for property that its creator, Mr. Gaston Hubot du Rivault, owned in Poitou.

Fairly large, it measures 24 to 28 inches. It is a well-built dog, strong yet svelte, with the forequarters somewhat higher than the hindquarters. Its finely featured head has long flat ears that turn somewhat inward. Its short hair is rough to the touch, often on the thick side, and makes for a pleasant coat that is usually uniformly white or coffee-white. In some cases the coat can be off-white or faintly spotted with orange or yellow. This is a deer-hunting dog.

Chantelouve, seen here with Patrick Le Roux, is a member of the Point du Jour team. Mr. Michel Le Roux, its owner, is very attached to this beautiful French breed. He and a few other hunters saved this breed from extinction; their efforts were a vital contribution to the preservation of France's canine heritage.

BLUE GASCONY HOUNDS

The Blue Gascony hound descends from a breed known as the St. Hubert. These black dogs were bred originally by the Comte de Foix, Gaston Phébus, who established the line by crossing a number of different hunting breeds that no longer exist. Created during the Middle Ages, they are among the oldest breeds of French hunting dog, and they have changed little since the fourteenth century. This breed is remarkable for being daring, dynamic, enthusiastic and tenacious. The breed is divided into four different groups, each notable for its black and white speckled coat that gives it a bluish slate-gray appearance.

BLUE GASCONY GRIFFON

This dog is a cross between a gray wirehaired griffon and the Blue Gascony hound. It stands 17 to 21 inches at the shoulder, and is solidly built. Its coarse wiry coat lies mostly flat along the body except at the legs and on the chest where it is slightly curly. Gary, who belongs to Mr. Allain, is a fine example of the breed.

LARGE BLUE GASCONY HOUND

This breed averages between 26 to 30 inches in height, has a long pronounced head, a well-developed chest, a long sloping back and a rich coat that is not too short. Mr. Jacques Baylac has every reason to be proud of Cartouche, who is four years old and a superb example of the breed. True to the breed, he has a fine throaty bark that he employs only during the hunt—with the exception of certain special occasions. Indeed, Cartouche likes to sing along while Mr. and Mrs. Baylac play the accordion. Cartouche is especially fond of this instrument, which he accompanies in close rhythm with the melody. His singing progressively increases in volume and subtly changes in tone and pitch in near-perfect harmony with Mr. and Mrs. Baylac's playing.

Small Blue Gascony hound

The Small Blue is 21 to 24 inches tall and possesses a fairly long head that is somewhat more delicate than that of its larger cousin, the Blue Gascony hound. The length of its chest significantly exceeds its width; its back is somewhat long, and its coat is medium, not too short, and plush. Baron du Grand Veilly, shown here with Mr. André Lecomte but owned by Mr. Lionel Sourbets, is an excellent specimen of this breed, one of the oldest in France.

Blue Gascony basset

This dog measures 14 to 17 inches at the shoulder. The head is identical in all of its proportions to the Blue Gascony hound. The coat is somewhat coarse but rich in texture. The dark brown eyes and gentle look of Ceasar, owned by Mr. Daniel Gibert, are typical of this breed. It is said of the breed that the "dog has four eyes, two of which are marked by a fiery vibrancy," which means that the two patches of tan-colored fur above the eyebrows make the dog look like it has four eyes.

GRIFFON VENDEEN

The name "Griffon Vendeen" pertains to four different breeds that all issue from a large hunting griffon. The latter is a descendent of the white dogs bred by the royals or perhaps the Royal court dog, a variety itself of the royal white dog. These dogs were crossed with the gray Saint Louis breed, the Bresse griffon and the Fawn Brittany griffon to yield the Great Griffon Vendeen. The name "griffon" was given to these dogs because of their long, scruffy coats—the hair being very tangled. These breeds are notable for their intelligence and determination. They have long, fine, narrow ears. The back is slightly elevated and the tail is extended and frayed, with the hair on the tail resembling the barbs on a stalk of wheat. The coat is composed either of one color, such as light brown, gray, tan or white, or of two or three colors. This is a vigorous, courageous, loyal and unwavering animal, possessed with a keen sense of smell and a powerful bark.

MEDIUM GRIFFON VENDEEN

The Medium Griffon Vendeen is a slightly smaller hunting dog than the breed from which it is derived. It stands at 20 to 22 inches at the shoulder, between the larger breed and the basset. It is able to hunt all of the larger game. The elegant silhouette of Douchka de la Combe de Trousse-boi deserves the admiring gaze of Marion Fabre (preceding double page).

GREAT GRIFFON VENDEEN

This dog measures 24 to 26 inches at the shoulder. It is adept at hunting all wild game.

Dingo, who belongs to Daniel Boursier, epitomizes the breed's power, nobility and well-balanced proportions. This breed is distinguished by its devotion and steadfastness as a hunting dog.

ENGLISH FOXHOUND

This English hunting dog descends from a number of different local breeds, who were themselves bred not for their build but for their ability to hunt foxes. The dogs do not officially qualify as belonging to the breed until it has been confirmed that they are descended from at least six generations of foxhounds who have actively and exclusively hunted foxes. These are solid, durable dogs with strong constitutions. They have a powerful build, large skull, long neck, large back and a tail that must taper off. They hunt foxes in the open in an orderly, disciplined pack.

Caporol was born in England. Mr. Marcel Thépault has already completed numerous hunting seasons with Caporol and expects to see several more with his longtime companion, who, although ten years old, still retains all of the physical and temperamental qualities of the breed (above).

Anglo-Français de Petite Vénerie

As was the case for the larger Anglo-French breeds, this breed is the product of an astute cross between French and English breeds, a cross intended to combine the best hunting qualities of both. This dog was specifically bred to hunt rabbit. The best description of this dog is given by Dr. Emile Guillet, a superb connoisseur and defender of all French hunting breeds: "This small, compact dog is a half breed that is well-equipped for its purpose. It lives up to the elegance and distinction that mark the French breeds. It is solid, rapid and has good stamina. The nose and throat are typically French, but what best characterizes it in relation to other breeds of its size is its temperament. It has an excellent temperament for hunting large game, and moreover it is a clever dog that is easy to train." The dog is 19 to 22 inches tall. The coat is short, tight and smooth and composed either of three colors (white, black and tan) or just two (white and black, or white and orange). Edile, three years old, belongs to Mr. Alain Dubois and is a remarkable specimen whose characteristics would have delighted Dr. Guillet.

Beagle-harrier

The beagle-harrier was created in the late nineteenth century by French hunters. It is a cross between the harrier-beagle and the French Medium Griffon Vendeen. Over the years, the original line was found unsatisfactory, and newer lines were created by crossing beagles and harriers. These were developed according to a rigorous breeding scheme introduced by Professor Théret, who holds the Chair of Zootechnology at the École Nationale Veterinaire of Maisons-Alfort. The Central Canine Society approved the scheme, and the breed was officially established in 1980.

Etoile de la Vallée des Acacias, Flash de la Vallée des Acacias, Bora de Pauzat and Briska de Pauzat belong to Mr. Paltor. They are harmonious, well-built dogs with balanced features. They have medium-sized heads and wide, medium-length, almost flat ears.

The beagle-harrier has a somewhat short, thick coat that is smooth and generally made up of three colors. A multipurpose dog, it can hunt rabbit as well as fox, deer and wild boar.

ARTOIS HOUND

This old and rare breed, which descended from the bloodhound, almost disappeared in the twentieth century. About twenty years ago, a few aficionados decided to reconstitute the breed from a few remaining specimens, which they managed to locate after a long search. Thanks to them, the modern Artois hound closely resembles the original.

Measuring 22 to 23 inches at the shoulder, it is a well-constructed dog with a slow, graceful gait. It has a large, strong head, a medium-length back and a pointed tail that is somewhat long and sickle-shaped. Today, it is used primarily to hunt rabbit, although its ancestors were used to hunt deer.

At three years old, Elégante belongs to the Saint-Louis team. Mrs. Josette Pilat has every reason to be proud of Elégante. She is endowed with all of the physical and temperamental characteristics of her medieval ancestors.

PORCELAINE

This breed was created in the eighteenth century by hunters from Lorraine. It probably descends from the royal white dog and Swiss hunting dogs of the period.

By the 1970s the breed had become so rare that a club was created to preserve it. Its first task was a complete and systematic accounting of all extant members of the breed. The purpose was to identify the best specimens to be used in reviving the breed. The careful, controlled breeding of the line, which included a slight infusion of harrier and Billy blood, rapidly bore results: the breed's population regained its former levels.

Three-year-old Elan is shown here with its owner, Didier Barrier. It's clear that this small-game hunting dog is very distinguished, with qualities that make it exceptional in its group. Its rather long head sports fine fleshy ears. It has a fairly long neck, a wide, straight back and a medium-length tail that is slightly curved and tufted at the end. The coat is short, tight, fine and shiny. It is normally white with round orange spots. With a keen sense of smell and an excellent bark, the Porcelaine can hunt anything, but it is best at hunting rabbits.

FAWN BRITTANY HOUND

This is another of the oldest hunting breeds that were prominent during the Middle Ages. It is descended from a Brittany hunting dog that was a remarkable wolfhound. The breed was for a long time divided into three subtypes: the griffon, medium-sized and the basset (page 192). The medium-sized line has completely disappeared. The Fawn Brittany hound, bony and muscular, gives the impression of vigor and hardiness. Its ears are medium-length and pointed, its neck is muscular, its chest large and tail long and slightly curved. The coat is coarse and wiry, thick but not too long. The color of the coat varies from golden-red to brick-red.

FAWN BRITTANY GRIFFON

This dog stands between 19 and 22 inches at the shoulder and is used to hunt wild boar and foxes. Bob, who belongs to Mr. Conn, is tough, active and full of character. Endowed with an excellent temperament, it can endure all sorts of hardship, and its hardiness makes it adaptable to all terrains.

GRIFFON NIVERNAIS

This old French breed probably descends from the Bresse griffon that no longer exists. Popular for several centuries, its numbers dwindled during the second half of the eighteenth century. Fortunately, concerned breeders joined forces to revive it, and their plan was successful.

The Griffon Nivernais is a "barbed" hirsute dog with a coarse coat. It measures 22 to 24 inches at the shoulder. Its head is somewhat long, and it has supple, somewhat hairy medium-length ears. Its back and tail are extended. The coat is wolf-gray or blue-gray or black. The coat is otherwise tan around the jowls, above the eyes and at the extremities. Courageous, if somewhat sad looking, this dog has an exceptional build meant more for endurance than speed. Mr. Guy Lamoureux and Alain Jullien, who own Gonfleur and Fanfare, are never short on praise for these two dogs, whom they appreciate for their keen sense of smell, their superb retrieving qualites and their enthusiasm in the field. They note that the Griffon Nivernais is especially suitable for hunting wild boar or fox.

Fawn Brittany basset

At 13 to 15 inches tall, this dog is basically a miniature Fawn Brittany hound whose back is proportionally longer. This dog is used to flush out wild game. Aster and Dick, trained to hunt rabbit, have a coarse, tough coat that allows them to penetrate the densest thickets and underbrush. Quick and tenacious in action, they give Mr. Robert Monard complete satisfaction back at home due to their calm, affectionate natures.

Small Basset Griffon Vendeen

This small dog, 14 to 15 inches tall, is remarkable for its speed. When let loose on its own in a medium-sized field, the Small Basset Griffon Vendeen is the superlative assistant to any hunter of pheasant or rabbit. It is also an excellent companion with an expressive face and charming manner. Dalton, Eglantine, Emma, Bulle, Gazelle and Houra are the perfect family dogs, as the Fauchereau family can attest. These six little hunters allow the children of the family to pull their tails, their hair and their whiskers without complaint.

BASSET–ARTÉSIEN–NORMAND

This breed was created in the nineteenth century by crossing a Basset d'Artois with a Basset Normand. Ermine des Compagnons des Hautes Erres, who belongs to Mr. Christian Dubois, demonstrates the basic basset qualities. The athletic build is elegant and graceful.

The Basset Artésien Normand is 12 to 14 inches tall. Its dome-shaped head is adorned with fine, long fleshy ears. Its chest is wide and round, and its back is well-suspended. Its long tail progressively tapers off toward the end and is at times extended. The coat is short and composed either of two or three colors. It has a very keen sense of smell, sticks close to the trail and has a fine bark. It is adaptable to all types of wild game but is best suited for rabbit and wild hare. Its gentle temperament, obedience and devotion make it an agreeable companion.

LARGE BASSET GRIFFON VENDEEN

This line was established by Mr. Paul Desamy, who wanted a breed whose size permitted it to pursue and catch wild hare. They are 16 to 17 inches tall.

Mr. Guy Raffier often hunts white hare in the Briançonnais at high altitudes with his dog Uxel and Uxel's offspring Don Juan des Hautes Clauzes (right). He loves the sight and sound of the pack as it wanders the terrain flushing out the white hare.

HARRIER

This English dog was bred, as its name indicates, to "harry" wild hare during the hunt.

Several local varieties first appeared during the Middle Ages. English hunters standardized the breed in the nineteenth century. The great cynologist Emile Guillet thought the dog had an average sense of smell and a poor temperament for hunting. He found that the dog lacked initiative and had an erratic bark. In his opinion, the dog was best suited for fox hunting in open terrain rather than in thick underbrush.

Over the years, the dog has benefited from French breeding, and now are superlative hunters of wild hare. They are sometimes used to hunt fox, deer and wild boar in difficult terrain.

Velina de la Petite Roche, to the right of Mr. Jean-Claude Maeso, has a strong yet light build (page 196). She has a medium-large head, a long, slightly pointed muzzle and somewhat short, V-shaped ears. The harrier has a smooth, flat coat. The coat is off-white with a spectrum of shades ranging from black to orange. In France the coat is often composed of three colors.

BEAGLE

Although its origins remain controversial, we do know that the beagle was brought to France in the eleventh century to hunt wild hare. Two types exist in England: the first is the standard beagle, which is unsuitable for hunting; the second is an excellent hunter, but its build does not conform to the standard type. The French beagle club has undertaken to create a variety that satisfies the standard form and can also hunt. Their attempts have been very successful. The beagle has a short, thick coat. It is composed of just about all colors typical of hunting dogs with the one constant being that the tip of the tail is always white. Derby de la Petite Roche, to the left of Jean-Claude Maeso, is quick, active, vigorous and distinguished. Its head is strong without being too heavy, and its ears are flat and round at the tips. Like many lovers of hunting dogs, Mr. Maeso does not use a gun when he takes the dogs out to hunt. Rather, he just enjoys watching and listening to the "music "of the dogs as they seek out and chase game across the countryside.

HARRIER

See caption on page 194.

BASSET HOUND

This British dog is descended from the Basset d'Artois; several types of these dogs were brought to Britain where they were crossed with beagles and bloodhounds. This is the heaviest set of all the bassets. Short legged but well-proportioned, the basset has an appearance of distinction despite its heavy frame. Its size varies from between 13 to 15 inches, and it weighs between 55 and 66 pounds.
As we can see from David of du Clos d'Egremont and Flotentin d'Egrement, who belong to Mrs. Geneviève Nicolas, the basset has a characteristically large head with a dome shaped skull and heavy folds of skin. Its brown eyes are gentle and sad-looking. The body is long with a fairly wide back. The coat is normally made up of three colors (black, tan and white). Its real forté is hunting, especially foxes, wild boar and wild hare. Indeed, despite its dumpy appearance, the breed is quite agile.

SCHWYZ HOUND

White is the background color of this dog's coat, which usually has large spots that are colored bright orange, yellow orange or reddish orange.

Five medium-sized Schwyz hounds and a puppy, Filou du Val Durance, are gathered around Mr. Jean-Michel Caponi. With them is Ecume des Sources de Kervelen who is sitting on Jean-Michel's shoulder. This latter dog reminds him of an adventure of sorts that befell one of his Schwyz hounds, Wolga, whom he often brings with him while traveling on business. Wolga, who is gifted with an exceptionally keen sense of smell, would take advantage of the frequent stops on the road to sniff out wild hare. One day, in the Alpes de Haute-Provence region in southern France, Mr. Caponi saw Wolga return with a downtrodden look. After a careful examination of the dog, he found the two marks of a viper's bite. He figured that given the size of the dog he had about an hour to get the dog to a vet before it died. He rushed off to Barcelonette in the car, only to get caught in a traffic jam just on the outskirts of town. He took the dog in his arms, got out of the car and dashed to the vet's, which was on the other side of town. Ten minutes later and completely out of breath he made it to the doorstep of the clinic and handed the already unconscious dog over to the vet murmuring the word "viper … viper." Wolga recovered a half hour after the antidote was administered, and Mr. Caponi will never forget the look in his eyes, still a little troubled but full of affection as he wagged his tail.

POINTERS

In the Middle Ages, the ancestors of these dogs were used to locate birds and to mark where they were in the bush, usually by lying down and pointing in the right direction. Once the birds were located the hunters would arrive and throw nets over the birds from behind the dogs. That is how the dogs became known as setters.

The role of the "byrde dog"—as it was originally known—was at first fulfilled by shorthaired dogs known as "brachet." The role was next turned over to dogs of medium-length hair that were trained to *s'espaigner,* which means to lie flat on the ground, once they had found the game. The verb *s'espaigner* was first mentioned in the Book of Hunting written in the fourteenth century by Gaston Phébus, and it is the etymological origin of the word "spaniel."

A long time ago, bird dogs were used to find game, which was then hunted by bow and arrow and later by crossbow. Finally, they were trained to mark the spot where the game was and to crouch down and indicate with their muzzles a bird's exact location.

This seventh category is made up of two groups. The first includes breeds from the European continent, which are further divided into three subgroups depending on the kind of coat they have. The pointing dogs are shorthaired dogs. The spaniels are longhaired or medium-longhaired dogs with silky coats, and the griffons are medium- to longhaired dogs with coarse wiry coats.

The second class includes those breeds that are originally from the British Isles: shorthaired pointers and the longhaired setters. These breeds were created after the continental breeds and are the result of a cross between the continental dogs and more local breeds. The continental breeds were first introduced to Britain in the sixteenth century.

ITALIAN BRACCO

Dea de Cascina Merigo, who belongs to Mr. William Courrance, belongs to one of the oldest, if not the oldest, breed of Mediterranean pointer. This breed was a favorite with nobility during the Renaissance. In the nineteenth century, the breed became a lot heavier than its ancestors, and earned the reputation of being rather sluggish hunters. A strict selective breeding program solved the problem and restored the breed to its more lithe form. For over forty years, breeders have been careful to use only the fastest dogs for maintaining the breed. Thanks to these efforts, today's pointer has a long graceful, galloping gait. The dog is resilient and has good stamina, which makes it perfect for hunting all types of game, both birds and animals, on all kinds of terrain.

A well built dog of about 27 inches and 88 pounds, it has a powerful neck and muscular legs, which give it an appearance of great vigor. Its tail is bobbed. Its coat is short and shiny, usually white with either brown or orange spots.

GERMAN WIREHAIRED POINTER

This breed was created in the early twentieth century by German breeders who were determined to put an end to the dominance that English hunting breeds enjoyed. To achieve that end, they crossed the pudelpointer, the stichelhaar, the airedale and the German pointer. The drahthaar, a coarse-haired dog, was the result of that cocktail and came into being shortly before World War I. It stands an average of 26 inches at the shoulder and is notable for its tight, thick, wiry hair which provides it with the perfect protection. This is a well-proportioned and distinguished looking dog with the length and the height of the body being about equal. Its dark brown coat is mixed with white and gray patches. Its clear, sad eyes are deeply set in their sockets. The protective attitude that Cyrus des Marais de Courmont has toward his master Mrs. Lainé, along with his energetic and proud disposition, underscores two of the drahthaars principal personality traits: fidelity and vitality.

WEIMARANER

Dog lovers are not in complete agreement about this dog's origins. Some say the dog descends from a medieval gray French dog, several of which were owned by French King Saint Louis. After the French stopped raising the breed, the dukes of Weimar took over. Others say the breed is a cross between the German pointer and other diverse breeds, and was created uniquely by the dukes of Weimar. But everybody agrees that it was the dukes of Weimar who are responsible for establishing the splendid color of its coat.

With its moderately elongated head and its large ears, ample chest, long back and solid muscular build, this dog appears to be graceful and robust. It stands about 24 to 28 inches tall. This excellent pointer is also a remarkable retriever.

There are two different varieties: Barthélemy, Daphné du Dolmend de la Noeveillard and their daughter Gertrude, shown here with Mrs. Catherine Buel-Gromaire, belong to the shorthaired variety that is characterized by a fine, dense coat. The second variety is characterized by a coat that is long, soft and silky (following double page).

LONGHAIRED
WEIMARANER

Ehla and Ekkla, with amber eyes highlighted with silver tints, belong to Mr. Bruno Fasoli. The hair "sticks out "on these dogs and is about 1 to 2 inches long. This variety is also distinguished by a slightly shorter tail.

BOURBONNAIS POINTER

Part of France's national heritage was saved by the concerted efforts of a group of breeders who were very attached to this regional breed. This dog is the result of a judicious selection procedure and was bred from a variety of ancient continental pointers.

The reconstitution of the two original colors of the Bourbonnais pointer caused the breeders considerable trouble. The coat, which is short and thick, can be "peach flowered" (fawn with white speckles) such as the coat of Elbrouk de la Bénigousse, or "wine colored" (brown with white speckles), such as those of Extra du Pontel de Maicou, Folie de la Bénigousse and Gentiane du Pontel de Maicou, all

four of whom belong to Mr. Patrice Mallet. Measuring 22 inches at the shoulder, this dog, which has a slightly convex shaped back, is usually born without a tail. Sometimes, however, the dog is born with a short tail. This light dog is a methodical hunter and usually moves at a gallop. It is best suited for bird hunting, particularly for woodcock and snipe.

GERMAN SHORTHAIRED POINTER

The German shorthaired pointer was created in the second half of the nineteenth century. Its ancestors were Mediterranean pointers that were later crossed with local breeds. Finding the dog a bit slow, breeders in the early twentieth century tried to lighten the dogs by crossing them with Doberman pinschers.

Waiting attentively at the feet of Mrs. Maly Taravel and ready for action, Alto and his sons Drilling and Delta, each certified by the office of Clos de Luenas, are powerful, graceful athletes whose fine builds guarantee energy, endurance and speed.

The German shorthaired pointer is about 26 inches tall. Its coat is tight and short as well as coarse. It is usu-

ally brown or brown and speckled white, and sometimes it can be black or black and speckled white. Its eyes and nose are brown. It also has round medium long ears that fall around the jowls. This is a bird hunting dog that is at home either in the field, the woods or the marshes.

FRENCH POINTER

This dog is descended from the bird dogs of the Middles Ages, the ancestors of all the breeds in this category. There are two varieties of French pointer, both of which are able to hunt for long periods of time over difficult terrain. They are adept at hunting quail, pheasant, partridge and wild hare.

GASCONY TYPE

This is the largest of the two extant types at 23 to 29 inches. Its head, large but not especially heavy, has medium-long ears that are round and folded at the ends. Its neck is the perfect length; the back is straight, and the tail is bobbed. The coat, thick and plush, is brown or brown and white, or brown with fawn spots.

Anky des Messugues Feuries loves to eat. He has been banned from entering the kitchen, where he is liable to make a mess despite the normally good behavior of the French pointer. When the odor of cooking wafts his way, it is all that Mr. Jean-Pierre can do to keep him from rushing into that forbidden place.

PYRENEAN TYPE

Buck du Clos Michaud, who belongs to Mr. Jean Pierre Coeurdray, demonstrates that the Pyrenean variety has exactly the same proportions and characteristics as the Gascony type. But it differs in size—it is about 2 inches smaller. Its jowls are also less droopy, the ears hardly at all folded and its coat shorter and finer—not to mention its tail, which is also thinner.

HUNGARIAN SHORTHAIRED POINTER

The Hungarians assert that their national pointer comes from a primitive Hungarian hunting dog, the Pannonie, and a yellow Turkish. Later, the breed was crossed with several other hunting breeds and standardized in the late nineteenth century. An elegant, medium-sized dog of about 24 inches, it has a short fawn coat. Its face is sharp featured, and it has medium length, V-shaped ears. Its back is short and straight. The tail is generally bobbed to about a quarter of its natural length. This dog is calm by nature, has a keen sense of smell and is adaptable and resilient. It makes for an affectionate companion, which is just what Apache de la Bétoule is to his daughter Etna.

Mr. Rochereuil was deeply embarrassed when he entered Apache in the world game-hunting championships. During the retrieval competition, Apache jumped into the water and swam toward the bird, but instead of grabbing it, he just swam around it in circles. Mr. Rochereuil then realized that Apache had never seen a duck before.

ARIEGE POINTER

This dog descends from a French breed, the St. Germain pointer. This is an old breed from southwest France, and it almost disappeared prior to World War II. Fortunately, a couple of dog breeders decided to revive the breed from a few of the remaining specimens whose characteristics still conformed faithfully to the original. The position assumed by Mr. Alain Deteix, that of a sprinter on the block, expresses his determination to complete the revival of this part of France's national heritage. He has been put in charge by the Bureau of Fish and Game, in accordance with the Central Canine Society, of overseeing the breed's recovery. Gouar de la Vallée de la Justale

seems to be enjoying himself. The Ariège pointer is about 26 inches tall. It is solidly built, with a wide, deep chest, a back that is slightly convex in shape and a white coat with brown or orange spots—all features that lend the dog a lot of character. It is suited to hunting partridge or wild hare.

ITALIAN WIREHAIRED POINTER

This dog's precise origins are still unknown. This is a large dog (28 inches), solid, rustic and vigorous. As we can see from Happiness Fanny, who is standing beside his master, Mr. Hugues Perronny, the head of the dog is bearded and the ears are medium length and triangular in shape. Its neck is strong and muscular. Its coat, made of rough, tight and lightly curly hair, is usually white, white with orange spots or brown. This is an all-terrain hunting dog. The tough coat means that it is at home in thick underbrush and in marshes, even when the water is very cold. When it hunts, it moves with an ample, quick trot that can turn into a pleasant gallop at times. This is an all-purpose hunting dog.

PORTUGUESE PERDIGUEIRO

Its ancestor was an ancient Mediterranean pointer. This breed has developed considerably over the centuries. The breed is not well known in France, and Taro do Odelouca, who belongs to Mr. Rochereuil and Mrs. Marquet, is one of the first introduced into France.
The dog is 22 inches tall and weighs 60 pounds. The Portuguese pointer has an excellent build, which endows it with considerable agility. Its has a rather small head and medium-length ears that are rounded at the ends. The neck is somewhat long, the back, short, and the hindquarters, fairly squat. The coat is short and stiff and normally a uniform yellow-brown but sometimes spotted.

BURGOS POINTER

This is one of the oldest pointing breeds, but its origins remain unknown. Ton, who belongs to Mr. Pascal Moreira, is of average size for his breed—about 26 inches—and of medium build; this dog gives an impression of power and hardiness.

The Burgos pointer has a large, solid head with long dangling ears. The look in its chestnut eyes is gentle and slightly melancholy. The coat is tight, short and smooth. It is normally white with liver-colored spots. The tail is bobbed to about one-third to one-half its natural length. This dog is suited both for fowl and wild game. Its favorite prey is the partridge. In action, its gait is long, powerful and efficient.

ST. GERMAIN POINTER

The breed was created in the mid-nineteenth century by crossing French pointers with other pointing breeds. Its initial popularity (Napoleon III and a number of other dignitaries from his court owned a few) later diminished considerably. Nevertheless, this elegant, well proportioned dog deserves the popularity it enjoyed in former times.

Dic du Bois d'Heilly, who belongs to Mr. Stanislas d'Argentre, has large golden-yellow eyes, which give the breed its frank and gentle appearance. This is a very well-tempered dog who loves to express his true nature as a retriever, often pouncing on any object that can be brought to its master—toys, sticks and small rocks.

The ears of the St. Germain are smaller than the older breed, the French pointer, but longer than that of the other pointing dogs from which it is descended. The neck is fairly long, the chest is wide and the back is short and straight. The fur is short and never coarse, while the coat itself is off-white with orange spots.

BLUE PICARD SPANIEL

This breed is a cross between a Picard spaniel and a Gordon setter. It became an official breed in its own right during the period between the two World Wars. Attila de la Valée de l'Ysieux, who belongs to Mr. Lucien Bernard, is a perfect example of the breed.

The Picard blue has a low-set build, and its appearance is very similar to the Picard spaniel except that its hair is flat and wavy, and a speckled gray-black color. Its fur is magnificent, and its bluish tint gives the dog's shape a more rustic aspect than that of the Picard. It measures 24 inches and has an attractive head framed by somewhat thick ears that are beautifully fringed. Its back is fairly short. Its legs are also well furnished with tassel-like fur. Tireless and good-tempered, this dog can hunt most game. Its keen sense of smell makes it an excellent hunter of woodcock.

BRITTANY SPANIEL

Among its ancestors was a small dog that lived in Brittany during the twelfth century. The descendents of this dog were used in the nineteenth century by woodcock hunters from Argoat. When they were crossed with hunting dogs from the British Isles, the result was the Brittany spaniel, whose exceptional qualities quickly earned it a formidable reputation. This little dog is completely fearless. It is quick and intelligent, dynamic and always alert. Flicka de Saint-Tugen and Caouette de Saint-Tugen are always ready when Mr. Maurice Marchand gives them the call.

It stands a maximum of 20 inches, and has a round head and a muzzle with elevated lips. Its ears are short and somewhat fringed. Compact and stocky, it has a straight back and relatively round features. The tail varies in size from very short to fairly long.

The coat is either straight or wavy and colored white and orange, white and brown, or black and white. This is one of the most popular French hunting dogs. It has an excellent sense of smell, is tireless and can endure all conditions and climates. Its ability to hunt in all kinds of terrain makes it adaptable to hunting a variety of game, and its small size affords it certain advantages.

MÜNSTERLÄNDER

Cook du Clos des Hortioux, seen here mischievously perched above his master, Mrs. Geraldine Roos, hasn't a clue that the breed he belongs to, though only recognized between the two World Wars, has in its ancestry a German bird dog. The Münsterländer comes in two varieties, which have a few features in common, such as an aristocratic head, a deep chest and a straight back. The dog is at home on all types of terrian and can hunt any kind of game. It is notable for being a methodical stalker.

The large Münsterländer stands 22 to 23 inches tall in comparison with the smaller variety, which stands 20 to 22 inches tall. The coat is white with black or maroon spots, while the smaller of the two has a coat that is white and brown or brown-maroon.

GERMAN LONGHAIRED POINTER

Although this breed dates back several centuries, it was eschewed by German hunters in favor of the German pointer and the drahthaar. Today, the breed is enjoying something of a comeback in its native land but is still largely unknown outside Germany. Capone du Buisson de Choisel hunts with Mr. Alfred Vallet in the Chevreuse valley, on the same land where members of the French royalty once hunted. He is seen here demonstrating how big this longhaired hunting dog actually is—about 26 inches. The dog is also robust and muscular, with an elongated head, and a straight, short back. Its long hair is straight and fringed at the paws. The coat is brown.

FRENCH SPANIEL

Although it descends from the bird dogs of the Middles Ages, the precise genealogy of this breed remains uncertain. On the other hand, it is known that this dog is the origin of several other breeds. Friendly and gentle, this is a loyal and devoted dog. This faithfulness explains the impatience with which Dervin rushes to join his master, Mr. Monceau de Lafitte, who divides his attention equally between Dervin and Titien.

The purity of this breed of dog is responsible for its pleasing, harmonious build. A medium-sized dog, it holds its well-sculpted head proudly. The dog's amber colored eyes reflect intelligence. Its coat is made up of straight fur that is silky and covers the body abundantly. It is white with irregular brown spots. This dog can hunt any kind of wild game, whether animal or fowl, over any kind of terrain, be it an open field or a marsh.

RETRIEVERS, FLUSHING DOGS AND WATER DOGS

This category includes breeds used for highly specific tasks. These tasks require a certain aptitude and breeding altogether different from the standard hunting breeds.

The first subgroup includes breeds used to retrieve wounded or dead game on land or in water. These dogs belong to breeds that are capable not only of retrieving small game such as woodcock and partridge but also larger game such as pheasant and wild hare.

Some of these breeds have highly specialized abilities, which make them adaptable to more unusual purposes. These abilities depend on certain qualities, in particular a keen sense of sight and smell, attentiveness, a good sense of direction, determination, courage and a gentle disposition. These qualities make them especially useful as seeing-eye dogs, dogs trained for aiding disabled individuals and dogs trained by the police and customs officials for detecting drugs and explosives.

The second subgroup includes dogs bred to detect and flush out wild game, whether it be in the field, in thick underbrush or in heavily wooded areas. They are often referred to by the term *broussailleur,* or bush dog. Originally they were bred only for the purpose of flushing out wild game. The job of pursuing and retrieving the game was reserved for other breeds. Today, most of these breeds are trained to undertake all three tasks.

The third subgroup includes those breeds that are specialized in hunting animals and water fowl either by the sea, along rivers or in swamps and marsh land. This type of game includes different varieties of water fowl, such as duck, waders (snipe, plover, curlew) and grouse and coot.

All the dogs belonging to these breeds love water. They take great pleasure in diving into water regardless of the temperature. That's because they have thick, multi-layered coats that adequately protect them from freezing temperatures.

LABRADOR RETRIEVER

Dance With Me de Saint-Urbain has adopted an attitude that demonstrates this breed's attachment to its masters, in this case Mr. Michel Germain. This social breed does not like being alone.

The breed is descended from the Saint-John which was brought to England from Newfoundland by English sailors at the end of the eighteenth century. The remarkable characteristics of this dog made it a favorite among English breeders, who for sixty years instituted a strict breeding program that included only the finest specimens. The breed was formally established only at the end of the nineteenth century. This dog is above all a hunting dog whose hardiness makes it adaptable to all sorts of game. It is a superb retriever, especially in water. A medium-sized dog, it is solidly built, compact and strong. The coat is short. The tail is medium length, tapered to a point and extended directly from the back. The color of the coat is black, brown or yellow. This active dog is known to be "gentle of tooth," as it retrieves game without damaging it.

FLAT–COATED RETRIEVER

This medium-sized breed is the product of a careful breeding program implemented in the late nineteenth century by British breeders, who wanted to create an English dog that specialized in retrieving wild game from all types of terrain. They crossed a North American breed from the region around the Saint Lawrence River with the Irish setter. The North American breed was chosen because of its strong build and its love of water.

The dog measures an average 24 inches in size and weighs about 75 pounds. It has an elongated head with a flat skull, small ears and a powerful jaw. Its coat is fine but thick and flat. The color is black or brown, and the paws and tail are heavily fringed. Active and alert, this is a natural-born hunter with a remarkably keen sense of smell. It is able to hunt on all kinds of terrain but is best in marshland, as it is an exceptional swimmer.

Its patience, obedience and lively disposition make it a wonderful companion, as Mr. and Mrs. Demon know from their experience with Life Spring du Bois de Flandre.

RHODESIAN RIDGEBACK

This dog is descended from a Rhodesian breed that was crossed with European breeds brought from Europe by the Boers. The result was this large South African dog that the Boers used to track lions, flush them out and chase them in the direction of the hunters.

Asimbothanda reveals the unique characteristic that gives the dog its name: a crest of hair that runs along the dog's back in the opposite direction from the rest of the coat.

Standing 27 inches tall, this large dog is strong, muscular, active and has excellent endurance. The dog accelerates rapidly and is remarkably calm during the chase. Asimbothanda didn't hesitate to jump 8 feet to join his master, Mr. Bruno

Hachet, to reach the roof where he was working.

Detached and intelligent, the Rhodesian ridgeback has an excellent sense of smell, which of course makes him a superb tracking dog, while his detachment makes him perfect for hunting wild boar and deer.

NOVA SCOTIA DUCK TOLLING RETRIEVER

The ancestry of this dog has not yet been precisely determined. The breed originated in Nova Scotia, a province of Canada situated off the Atlantic seacoast near the United States. The dog specializes in retrieving duck.

It is medium-sized—a maximum 20 inches for around 50 pounds—and has a compact and muscular body. Its head is notable for its large size, streamlined muzzle and triangular shaped ears of medium length. When in action, the tail is raised and rolled up. It has a double layered water resistant coat. The coat can be any shade of color ranging from red to orange. Despite a somewhat dumpy appearance, the dog is actually very agile. It is a determined and energetic duck hunter, and it stalks its prey with great speed. During the chase, it constantly wags its tail.

When not hunting, the dog is a great companion, as demonstrated by Ducky Ardunacres, who belongs to Mrs. Léveille-Nizerolle.

CHESAPEAKE BAY RETRIEVER

The origins of this dog are a matter of controversy among dog lovers. There are two different versions: some say the breed descended from a primitive North American breed that developed over the centuries. For others, the breed did not come into being until the nineteenth century and was the result of a cross between the Newfoundland and local Maryland breeds. Interestingly, Newfoundlands are thought to be the survivors of a shipwreck in the Chesapeake bay and were saved by the inhabitants of the region. What is certain, however, is that the Chesapeake Bay retriever is an excellent swimmer.

The dog is 23 to 27 inches in size and about 65 pounds. Like Chesabay Cruiser, called Duck, who belongs to Mr. Jean-Louis Pigal, these dogs have large round heads and small pendulous ears. The neck is very muscular, and its "wild hare feet" are webbed and large. Its coat, with short straight fur, can be any color, ranging from dark brown to light tan or even straw colored. It has an excellent sense of smell.

GOLDEN RETRIEVER

Despite the innumerable controversies surrounding the origins of this dog, it seems certain that this breed was created at the end of the nineteenth century by an English breeder who crossed flathaired retrievers with the Irish setter. Agile, with a great love of water, this is multipurpose hunting dog.

The disposition of this dog is calm and gentle, as we can see from Ugo Shildge, who lives in perfect harmony with his parents' three other retrievers: Uranie, Far West and Derby (above).

A medium-sized dog, the golden retriever is perfectly proportioned. Its head is distinguished by a snout that ends abruptly, a black nose, and ears that are medium-sized and floppy. The expression on its face is gentle and friendly. The coat is thick, with silky, straight fur. It paws are fringed, as is its tail, which falls directly from its back. The color of the coat ranges from cream to deep golden without any trace of red. Sunbeam Gentle V.H. Heideduin, who belongs to Mrs. Marja Kuyf-Jochemus, is seen below.

CLUMBER SPANIEL

The ancestors of this breed were British spaniels that were chosen for being heavy-boned. It owes its name to the Clumber Castle, which is located in the county of Nottingham. There, the dukes of Newcastel established a kennel that housed a large number of the breed.

Its long body is strong and low-set and this gives it the appearance of being massive and slow, which is not at all the case. This is, in fact, a very active dog. Measuring on average 19 inches and 72 pounds, it has a square-shaped powerful head with a wide brow. Its eyes are somewhat deep-set, which gives the dog a pensive air. The coat is abundant, tight and silky. The color is white with yellow marks. Due to its determination, the Clumber excels in finding wild game in heavy underbrush. Its stable disposition also makes it an agreeable companion.

Mr. Alain Jacq is rightly proud of Basile de Floriac, whose sire was the original stud used in breeding the French variety before he was hit by a car and killed.

AMERICAN COCKER SPANIEL

This breed was created in the twentieth century from the English cocker by American breeders who desired a smaller version of the dog with longer hair.

Eli-France du Clos d'Aldebaran, who belongs to Mr. Jean Diot but is seen here in the arms of Mrs. Pascale Cauche, is the epitome of this breed: he has a finely chiseled head with a foreshortened muzzle that makes the head look square in comparison to the English cocker. The fur is short and soft on the head, of medium length on the body and beautifully fringed around the ears, chest, stomach and paws. The tail is bobbed. The coat can be all one color, ranging from black to any other tint, or it can have two well defined and well separated colors.

Due to its graceful form, the American cocker is a true athlete, solidly built and endowed with a keen sense of smell. Rapid and tireless, this dog loves to hunt. It is also intelligent and "bubbly," its natural good humor and joyfulness making it a veritable clown. The dog is small enough to go anywhere and is a pleasant traveling companion. Lady, the heroine of the cartoon *Lady and the Tramp*, made this American breed enormously popular.

ENGLISH SPRINGER SPANIEL

This dog, which belongs to the large English spaniel family, was established by English hunters who desired a dog that would be able to hunt on all kinds of terrain. This is the largest spaniel bred to hunt in either the fields or woods. At 20 inches, it has a large, beautifully shaped and somewhat round head with finely fringed ears. The tail, also fringed, wags often, reflecting the dog's liveliness and love of life. The coat is straight and tight, protecting it from inclement weather, and colored either black and white or brown and white. It sometimes has three colors, with the third color being dark tan.

A natural-born hunter, this dog is large and solidly built, which means it can cover large areas with great speed, often creating the impression that it is flying over the land. Thanks to its powerful jaws, it is able to retrieve heavy or large game.

This docile dog is adaptable to all lifestyles. It is a great family dog, as one can see from Cleavehill Yorkshire Quest and Polk du Pigeonnier Bruyères, seen here in the arms of Etienne and Rénaud. These twins are obviously proud to show off these English springer spaniels, which belong to their mother, Mrs. Fabienne Courtel.

WELSH SPRINGER SPANIEL

This breed is the result of a careful breeding program implemented during the nineteenth century. It is a cross between diverse local breeds; the goal was to obtain characteristics that are specific to the Welsh springer: great endurance, courage and insurmountable energy, which make it a multipurpose dog. It differs from the English springer spaniel in its smaller size (by about 1 inch), its large floppy ears—as demonstrated here by Fidji, seen in the arms of Mathias Catala—and the color of its coat, which is bright red and white.

Quick, active and tireless, the Welsh springer is an enterprising breed. Although normally very obedient, Fidji often gives in to the urge for comfort by occupying the armchair in front of the television, a place usually reserved for the people of the house. But her natural curiosity often distracts her, causing her to abandon this coveted spot, such as when Mr. Catala enters the house, and Fidji rushes over to see what's happening.

PORTUGUESE WATER DOG

The build of the Portuguese water dog indicates its close kinship with the barbet, which is not surprising given that both breeds are derived from a Middle Eastern dog that was brought to Spain during the Arab invasion and occupation of the Iberian peninsula. This medium-sized dog is well constructed with a large head, broad chest, short back and tail that is tufted at the end. The coat is either long and lightly curled or short with tight cylindrical curls. The coat is usually uniformly black, like that of Nosferatu de Montalin, called Dann, but it can also be uniformly brown or white, or black and white or brown and white. Mr. Pierre Botijo de Oliveira would like this breed to be better known in France. He is seen here with Dann, who is a perfect example of the breed, in the pose that Portuguese sailors used when signaling to their dogs to fetch the fowl that had escaped from their nets.

Alert, impetuous and hardy, the Portuguese water dog has excellent vision and a keen sense of smell.

IRISH WATER SPANIEL

This breed is a cross between the Irish setter and standard poodles. The precise date at which the cross occurred has not been established. It was most likely after the French Revolution, during which many aristocrats emigrated to Ireland.

A medium-sized dog, its oily coat is made of thick curls, which resemble the fleece of a sheep. The coat is colored brown but of an unusual tint particular to the breed. Eliot des Monts de Caux has the characteristic head of the Irish water spaniel: a long muzzle that is somewhat square and pronounced, a dome shaped forehead covered in long curls that resemble a wig, a brown nose that is well developed, and very long round ears that hang around the neck. Enthusiastic, this dog is particularly adapted to hunting fowl, but it is also able to hunt other game. Even though Mr. Jean-Paul Vieublé trained Eliot to hunt water fowl, he was nevertheless surprised once when hunting by the banks of a river to see Eliot chase a rabbit. In the nick of time he shot the rabbit, and Eliot happily retrieved it in perfect condition.

COMPANION
AND TOY DOGS

This category includes breeds that were developed for purposes of companionship, rather than to perform a specific function. These dogs are bred to play the role of friend and confidant to their master, to provide comfort to the lonely and reassurance and affection to family members. Dogs in this category thus play a considerable and indispensable social service in our contemporary urban environments. Although the distinguishing feature of these dogs may be their small size, the main characteristic for which these dogs were bred was not a convenient morphology but rather an attentive and genial disposition. As Professor Raymond Triquet explains: "There is, of course, no one single type of lap dog. The dogs in this category resemble each other only in that they are readily amenable to providing their masters with the pleasure of their company."

HAVENESE BICHON

Is it because this is the largest of the Bichon breeds, at 14 and 20 pounds, that Maiden Effort's Velasquez is so happy to dominate her master, Mrs. Nicole Perchet? It is certainly not because this Havanese is a little despot. On the contrary: although this dog can be assertive, it nevertheless remains an affectionate and obedient companion. It has a large flat head with large dark eyes that are usually black and a tapered muzzle with flat cheeks. The coat is made of soft tufted fur that is slightly curled at the ends. Its coat is occasionally white but usually dark beige or light brown, like a cigar. That is why this dog, of Mediterranean origin and unusually fastidious, was named after the "Havana."

BICHON FRISÉ

This breed was created in France during the fifteenth century from a cross between the Maltese and the poodle. The breed was officially established in the sixteenth century during François I's reign. This was Henri III's favorite dog, and the breed was enormously popular among European nobility. It was at this time that the verb *bichonner,* or "dress up," was coined. It referred to the excessive care that noblewomen lavished on their dogs. The breed fell out of fashion after World War I but was revived after the end of World War II through the efforts of several French and Belgian breeders. As a result, the breed is officially recognized as being both French and Belgian.

This is a robust dog measuring about 11 to 12 inches and is noted for its proud, almost haughty disposition. It has expressive eyes and a jet-black nose and the ears hang down and are covered with fine curly fur. The fur elsewhere is also fine, silky and tightly curled; the coat is completely white in color but requires little maintenance.

Darling and Elfy de Kalfrety, along with Fougasse and Graffiti du Petit Orme, seen here with Mrs. Sylvie Dordet, testify to the Bichon's playfulness and love of life. The dog is always good-tempered.

BICHON BOLOGNESE

Descended from the Maltese, this Italian breed was a favorite of the Medici. It was widely popular throughout Italy during the Renaissance, after which its popularity declined, and the breed was increasingly forgotten. Today, for example, there remain even in Italy only a few specimens of the breed, and very few litters are born each year.

Its long white fur and abundant curls give many people the impression that the dog requires a lot of upkeep. Nevertheless, the beautiful coat of this small dog, who measures 11 to 12 inches tall and weighs about 6½ to 9 pounds, requires only a daily brushing to maintain its fine luster. This is a playful affectionate dog who is always alert and on guard when he senses that something is up—as one can see from Genepy du Mont-Aiquille, who belongs to Mrs. Laurence Fluchaud.

MADAGASCAR

A shipwreck off the coast of Madagascar sometime during the sixteenth century is at the origin of this breed from Madagascar. It turns out that the survivors had a few Maltese dogs with them for companionship. The sailors rescued the dogs and swam to shore, where the dogs later bred with local toy breeds. Their cotton-ball tail, and the fact that the breed emerged in a region near Tuléar, gave the breed the French version of its name, the Coton de Tuléar.

This is a small breed well suited for city living. It is 12 inches tall and weighs about 12 pounds. The head is triangular in shape and nicely coiffed. The dangling ears are thin, and the nose is jet black with flared nostrils. As evidenced by Diabolo Swing Five O'clock and Evinrude du Petit Dan, seated on the knees of Nathalie and Goran Brabani-Brkic, this dog has a marvelous pure white coat made of long, fine, slightly wavy fur.

This dog has an affectionate, playful character and is always in good spirits. The Madagascar is an active dog with an infectious love of life.

MALTESE BICHON

This breed is the oldest in the Bichon family. All other Bichon breeds are descended from this dog. The breed originated in Egypt and eventually spread throughout the Mediterranean. It was brought to the islands of Malta and Sicily by the Phoenicians. It is not known if the breed first arrived in Malta, as its name would indicate. The breed gained its widest popularity in Italy during the Middle Ages.

The dog is 8 to 10 inches tall and weighs $6^{1}/_{2}$ to 9 pounds. That makes it the smallest of the Bichon breeds. Thanks to Yvon Perrin, shown here holding Solitaire Abbyat du Fantôme von Harlekin at arm's length, we can see that this small dog has a long, thin body covered with very long, silky, shiny fur. This bestows upon the dog an elegant, if uniform appearance. Its long white coat requires regular brushing.

Like all the other Bichon breeds, the Maltese is obedient, affectionate and very alert.

LITTLE LION DOG

Mr. Wilfrid Vattement has appropriately placed Fhidias Samson de l'Ancien Relais on display in a pose that best reveals the figure of this breed, which belongs to the Bichon family.

Its fur is cropped in the same style as a poodle, with the tail ending in a tuft. The coat makes it look like a little lion. The fur is long and wavy and never curly. The coat can be any color, but white, yellow and black are the most common.

Lively, intelligent and affectionate, it alerts its master with a sharp continuous bark the second it senses danger.

POODLE

This French breed was developed in the Middle Ages and descends from the barbet, a bird dog. The poodle became a favorite among ladies of the French royal court in the seventeenth century. Later, the dog also became popular among the lower echelons of society and achieved its widest popularity in the nineteenth century. The breed then found favor in Anglo-Saxon countries, especially in the United States. There, it is one of the three breeds with the largest number of annually registered births, according to the American Kennel Club.

This is a harmoniously built, well-proportioned dog. The coat is characteristically curly, with abundant fine and wooly fur. Although somewhat rare today, there is a type of poodle known as the "cordé," after its almost rope like locks of nearly equal length. The coat is generally colored uniformly white, black, brown, apricot or gray. Originally bred as a hunting dog adapted to marshy terrain, the wonderful disposition of this dog, with its proverbial fidelity, so beautifully depicted in Hector Malot's novel, *Sans Famille,* along with its vivacity, dynamism, endurance, playful character and intelligence, have made the poodle the most popular French breed. There are four different types of poodle distinguished by size.

STANDARD POODLE
(18 to 23 inches)

We can understand, given the proud disposition of Charley Ston des Ducs de Bourbon, who belongs to Mrs. Brigitte Garon-Laurent, why so many owners of this breed often refer to it as the "royal poodle" (below).

Calynka, a large apricot-colored poodle, who belongs to Mrs. Ala-giraude, is seen here looking maternal with Help Me Golden du Chateâu de Mesne, who is two months old (next page).

Toy poodle
(under 11 inches; ideally about 10 inches)

Mrs. Christiane Couroux is the owner of two gray toy poodles: Darling P'tit Fluff du Castel de Christ'Dogs and Cochy de l'Orée de Sologne (above), as well as Bambi de l'Orée de Sologne (black male at right) and Efanie du Castel de Christ'Dogs (black female below).

BROWN TOY POODLE

E'Choco Punch Brown Star's, who belongs to Patrice Loray, was the winner of the world championship in 1991 in Berlin.

MINIATURE WHITE POODLE
(from 11 to 14 inches)
Darling White Morning belongs to Miss Audrey Setbon.

BLACK MINIATURE POODLE
Cinderella von der Hutzelsweiz belongs to Miss Ute Eberhard.

ORANGE MINIATURE POODLE
Dorthée de la Robinière and Mrs. Sylvie Marquis are both proud of Dolorès de la Robinière, who won the world championship in 1992 in Spain.

MEDIUM-SIZED POODLE
(from 14 to 18 inches)
The beautiful gray coat of Dylan de Schwarz Igloo, who belongs to Mrs. Jean-Pierre Leconte, gives the dog a rather sophisticated appearance. Yet this is a real outdoor dog who loves to run about the countryside and roll around in puddles. It also loves chasing other animals and romping alone or with other dogs. Dylan carefully watches his masters' two geese, ready to take action if the gander should attack Mrs. Leconte.

BRABANÇON

This dog's coat is colored either a uniform red or black and tan.

As Mr. Stéphane Segal demonstrates here with Daphné de la Romance du Mal Aimé, who belongs to Mrs. Marie-France Wall, the compact size of the brabançons makes it easy to take them anywhere. Their almost human expression also makes them irresistible.

HAIRLESS DOGS

It was for reasons of simplicity that the originators of the different categories of dog breeds established the category of the "hairless breeds." In fact, no single breed is completely hairless, and the dogs belonging to this category have a bit of fur on their heads and at the end of their tails.

MEXICAN HAIRLESS

Originally from Mexico, this is a very ancient breed. Its name was given to it by the Incas, who considered it the living incarnation of Xototl, the God of the Earth. Xototl's task was to accompany souls of the dead to their final destination. It is therefore somewhat paradoxical that given how much they venerated this breed, the Incas also considered the dogs to be something of a delicacy, which they served up enthusiastically during festivals.

This breed is almost completely hairless except for a few hairs on its head and at the end of its tail. The dog has a gracious disposition. Its skin is smooth and soft to the touch and is generally dark brown, elephant gray, gray-black or black. This is the only dog to perspire through its skin, which explains why it only rarely exposes its tongue.

The dog is very dignified and reserved among strangers. But one can see from B'Luna, seated here on the lap of Mr. Pierre Maisonneuve, that the Mexican hairless is by nature an outgoing, dynamic and sociable dog. This dog is perfectly suited to urban environments because it is remarkably clean and hardly ever barks.

CHINESE CRESTED DOG

The origins of the Chinese crested dog remain a mystery. We only know that it was brought to the United States in the nineteenth century by sailors aboard an American ship arriving from China. The dog owes its name to the toupet-like fur on its head and the fact that the ship came from China. There are two types.

POWDERPUFF WITH
VEIL COAT (SPARSELY HAIRED)

This dog's shape is identical to the hairless variety, but thanks to Gi'Yana du Gué de Launay, who belongs to Mrs. Isabelle Arnoult, it is clear this dog is covered with a silky coat that resembles a powder puff. The texture of Gi'Yana's coat inspired one visitor at the 1992 French Farm Show to exclaim: "Jeepers! That's a hairless dog that's been dressed up" (above).

HAIRLESS

Svelte and finely boned, this active graceful dog is 11 to 13 inches tall and weighs a maximum of 10 pounds. The body is completely hairless except for the head, the paws and the end of the tail. The skin can be either mottled or uniformly colored. The tuft of hair that characterizes this dog begins at the end of the muzzle and ends at the top of the neck (right).

When he took Gipez Kumar to the 1992 French Farm Show, Mr. Daniel Arnoult was dumbfounded to hear a visitor exclaim: "Look at that dog! What is the world coming to when a dog is sheared like a sheep? "This remark surprised him so much that he thought he'd see what it felt like to be as naked in public as these dogs are.

SHI TZU

The position that Dolmo du Domaine de Monderlay has assumed atop Mrs. Huax, reveals the tendency of the Shih Tzu to be a bit domineering at times. That's not all that surprising, given that this breed was created in the seventeenth century at the Imperial Court of China. This breed is a cross between the Lhasa apso, a gift from the Dalai Lama, and the Peking spaniel. The breed was maintained by the emperesses of China until 1908.

The dog is usually between 9 and 11 inches tall. The head is large and round, and the eyes are somber looking. The head is adorned with a bushy mustache and beard,

which are often groomed in the form of a clump of fur that dangles like a chrysanthemum. The fur is very thick and covers the whole body. It is usually long and straight and forms, at the tail, a long plume that is shaped like "the handle on a tea pot." This is a clean, active, well-adjusted and impish compan-

TIBETAN SPANIEL

This is one of the oldest of all dog breeds. It is descended from a primitive Asiatic spaniel, which was the predecessor of almost all of the small-sized Asiatic breeds. This breed was the companion of the Tibetan lamas and nobility, who greatly appreciated the dog's well-

balanced disposition, sociability and amusing airs, that can turn into sheer shenanigans.

English breeders developed an interest in this dog during the period between the two World Wars.

This is a small dog, about 10 inches high, weighing between 9 and 13 pounds. The body is slightly longer than it is tall. It carries its little head high. Its muzzle is truncated close to the face, and its ears are tufted and dangle around the head. The silky fur is medium long on the body and long on the hindquarters and tail. The backs of the paws are also well tufted. The coat can be any color. Djetjun de la Garde Adhémar, seen here next to Germain Gora, is a golden-colored male with a black

face, with one of the most characteristic traits of this breed: independence. When Mrs. Gora and the other Tibetans are returning from a walk, for example, Djetjun stands alone and walks apart from the pack. Like Djetjun, Florette des Yomainris (seated on top of Germain), Hazan and Hangzou des Yomainris (seated next to Germain) are alert and sure of themselves. A reticent breed, these dogs rarely bark.

CHIHUAHUA

This dog is descended from a primitive breed that accompanied the Toltecs when they settled in Mexico during the tenth century. The dog later met the same fate as the Aztecs, who maintained the breed, after the arrival of the Conquistadors during the sixteenth century. A few survived among the peasants in isolated areas of what is today the state of Chihuahua, next to the United States border. It was there that American breeders rediscovered the dog in the nineteenth century. They appreciated the breed and dubbed it the Chihuahua, after the state where it was discovered. The dog is reputed to be the smallest breed in the world, weighing from 2 to 2¹/₂ pounds.

Contrary to its fragile appearance and small size, this dog is alert, active and tough. It has no fear confronting dogs that are much larger in size. Its head is round, and its muzzle is short and somewhat pointed with a black nose. The tail is curled up on the back. There are two varieties of Chihuahua that differ only with respect to the fur. Mrs. Germaine Blondel is seen here holding one of each. On the left, Carino Desierto del Perro, a smooth-haired variety, with tight and shiny fur. This is the most common of the two types. On the right is Ellips l'Archevault, of the longhaired variety. The hair on this dog is characteristically long and slightly wavy. The coat can be any color.

LHASA APSO

This very beautiful photograph of Chakporis Calypso, who belongs to Mrs. Annick Laurent, recalls the quip made by the French writer Colette: "A dog is a ball of fur with a heart." The photograph also reveals the magnificent coat of the Lhasa. The coat is composed of abundant stiff fur that is long and straight. The fur on the head and tail is lush and falls over the eyes. The Lhasa probably descends, in part at least, from the Tibetan spaniel. Experts say that the Lhasa occupied a privileged place in the Tibetan monasteries because it could detect any suspicious sound due to its keen sense of hearing.
This small dog is much longer than it is tall. Its head is adorned with a

thick beard and mustache. The coat is either uniformly colored or multi-colored, ranging from white to black, although yellow and brown are the most common colors. Chakporis Calypso's coat is reddish brown. Mrs. Laurent spent years finding a Lhasa of this color.
Robust, friendly and active, this dog loves company and is extremely clean. The Tibetans appreciate the dog for its mountaineering instinct and even claim it can warn of impending avalanches.

DALMATIAN

This breed is probably the result of a mix between the bull terrier and the pointer. The dog was employed in teams and accompanied the horses and coaches that were used in the past for transportation. The invention of the automobile led to a decline in popularity of this "coach dog," but it made something of a comeback after World War II, mainly because of the incredible popularity of the film *101 Dalmatians.* This is a medium-sized, active and muscular dog. Its long powerful muzzle is offset by floppy ears that hang around the head. The dog has the broad chest of an endurance run-ner. The tail is slightly curved toward the body. The fur is short, stiff and shiny. The coat is white and notable for its well-defined spots, which that can be either black or brown.

Loyalty, patience and an easygoing temperament are the hallmarks of this breed. Mrs. France Le Mouël describes Dusty de la Mare aux Buis' behavior accordingly: "To live with a Dalmatian is to live with an aristocrat dressed in a robe of unparalleled beauty. This kind-hearted but stubborn animal is more human than dog and, to be sure, it is the best of companions."

TIBETAN TERRIER

The ancestors of this robust dog, which measures 15 to 16 inches tall, accompanied Tibetan lamas and Yak herders in the mountains. They also accompanied Asian nomads as they traveled toward Europe, thereby becoming the ancestors of several European shepherd breeds, including the Pyrenean shepherd.

This dog is muscular, stocky and has a powerful body. The fur is long and fine, sometimes wavy, and forms a lavish coat that can be any color except brown. This dog is friendly and spirited, especially with people it knows—as can be seen with Ard-gowing Damelsa, who belongs to Mrs. Round Vanlaer. He is shown here with Chrostiphe Chijou. This well-balanced breed is noted for its intelligence. On the other hand, the dog is mistrustful of strangers and quick to alert its master when it hears anything suspicious.

CAVALIER KING CHARLES SPANIEL

A very ancient breed, this dog was enormously popular in European courts in the sixteenth and seventeenth centuries. The name "King Charles" comes from the fact that the dog was a favorite companion of King Charles II of England in the seventeenth-century. The physiognomy of the breed was altered in the nineteenth century (see King Charles spaniel), and the original breed disappeared. After World War I, breeders attempted to create dogs that looked like the miniature spaniels depicted beside Charles II in numerous paintings from the period. They succeeded, and the new type of breed was dubbed the "Cavalier King Charles spaniel." This active, graceful dog differs from the King Charles spaniel in its facial features. The head is almost flat between the ears, the forehead is somewhat accentuated, the muzzle is tapered and the jaws are strong and perfectly articulated. The senses of sight and smell are particularly well developed in this breed. The dog has a friendly disposition. With an outgoing, adventurous personality, it is afraid of nothing.

Above are Benjy and Elgath des Marliviers and their puppies affectionately gathered around Mrs. Danielle Marchand. Left is Lillico Mulligan, who belongs to Mrs. Wendy Lhote.

KING CHARLES SPANIEL

During the second half of the nineteenth century, English breeders decided that the enormous popularity of the pug was due to its flat muzzle. Breeders of the King Charles spaniel started developing a variety that would have just such a flattened muzzle. It took them thirty years to achieve their goal, which may have been the result of an intensive breeding program or a mix between the breed and other flat-muzzled breeds such as the Pekinese or even the pug itself. The head is large and round, while the muzzle is square, very short and snubbed. The long pendulous ears are fringed, an essential characteristics of this breed. The dog measures 9 to 12 inches tall and weighs 8 to 14 pounds. Its long silky coat can be black and tan or might include colors referred to as "blenheim" (rich chestnut markings on a pearly white background) or "ruby" (pearly white with bright brownish streaks). The King Charles spaniel hates solitude. A refined dog, it can display a great deal of dignity when necessary. Tudormurst Royal Falcon and Dear Emma de Vilfloriane, seen here with Mrs. Sylvie Desserne, who is holding a younger King in her arms, have found a perfect moment to display the quiet and reserved airs so typical of this royal breed.

JAPANESE SPANIEL (CHIN)

Intelligent and gentle, this dog loves children and family life. Cho Cho, Ali and Fétiche, who bear the surname "du Midnight Sun," love to play, but they always remain well-groomed and retain an air of dignity that is typical of this breed (see preceding pages). Their ancestors originated in Korea and arrived in Japan during the eighth century. Ownership of the dog was restricted to Japanese nobles, and the breed was deliberately limited in order to preserve its rarity.

The Japanese spaniel is a very small dog that is normally about 10 inches high. The coat is lavish and made of long silky fur that covers the entire body except for the muzzle. The long coat contributes wonderfully to the magnificent profile of this animal. Its head is rather large and its small, floppy ears are triangular in shape and set wide apart. The tail is carried above the back.

The breed consists of two types that are distinguishable only by a difference in weight: one variety is less than 8 pounds while the other is between 8 and 13 pounds. The coats of both are either brown and white or black and white.

PEKINGESE

This breed originated in China at the time of Confuscious and was largely confined to the imperial palace. In 1860, during the sack of Peking, British soldiers captured four Pekinese, took them to England and offered them to Queen Victoria, the Duchess of Wellington and the Duchess of Richmond. The latter established a new line, known as the "Goodwood," the source for most of the current European lines. The breed was introduced to France during the twentieth century and became popular during the period between the two World Wars.

This is a small, well-proportioned and robust dog that weighs between 6^1/$_2$ and 11 pounds. The head is very large, flat and broad. The ears are long, floppy and fringed. The eyes are large and dark brown, and the muzzle is wrinkled, very short and very wide. The coat is opulent and can be almost any color except white and brown.

The dog is by nature loyal and gentle, and conceals a fiery temper beneath a calm, almost haughty exterior. That goes for Elie Beau Fou Chin, Genesim Woodoo Lilly, Butterfly and Thalassa du Jardin de Trèfles, not to mention Horn's Black Bird and Clémentine du Jardin de Trèfles, seen here in the arms of Mr. and Mrs. Dessauvages.

CONTINENTAL TOY SPANIEL

It was in Flanders that the first traces of this breed appeared in the fourteenth century. The dog was used for hunting back then. During the Renaissance, however, the breed became popular as a lap dog among the ladies of the courts of Europe. They appreciated its mischievous-looking face and its floppy ears. In France, the breed fell out of favor during the eighteenth century but was maintained in Belgium, where breeders developed a straight-eared variety. Today, the different lines are considered to be a single breed that is recognized to be both French and Belgian in origin. Robust and well-proportioned, the Continental toy spaniel has a fine expressive head, a body that is barely longer than it is tall, straight paws and a plumed tail that it carries above its back. The dog measures a maximum of 11 inches high and weighs between 4 and 11 pounds. The coat is colored white and tinted either black or fawn.

PAPILLON SPANIEL

Pepejas Zantussa and Sovereign Torndals, as well as their two puppies, Gold and Gary, seen here in the arms of Mr. and Mrs. Jean-Claude Maimberte, all have the surname "les Rouennaises du Petit Couronne." Their ears are erect and open, a trait typical of this version of the Continental toy spaniel.

PHALÈNE SPANIEL

Thanks to Miss Sandrine Yonnet, the droopy ears that characterize the Phalène spaniel are perfectly visible on Eden des Perles du Clos, who, like others of the breed, is very playful (preceding double page).

BOSTON TERRIER

This dog is descended from diverse breeds that were raised for organized dog fights throughout Europe and the United States in the early nineteenth century. In order to lighten the heavy-set bulldog, breeders crossed it with terriers. One of the resulting lines was brought to the United States, where it was crossed again with another breed, also derived from a mix between the bull dog and other terriers. The name comes the fact that the breeders were from the Boston area. This was the first officially recognized American breed.

Tel the French Connection at Damar, who belongs to Mr. Laurent Carniaux (above), exemplifies the Boston terrier, with his large head, short, square muzzle and small, well-kept ears. The hindquarters are round and the tail is straight. The coat is made of short, very fine and brilliant fur and colored black and white. The dog has a gracious and powerful gait, which give it a decisive allure. The dog is not aggressive but knows how to make its presence felt and never hesitates to intervene if it feels its master is in danger.

FRENCH BULLDOG

This breed was created in Paris around 1850 by aficionados of small breeds. The breed is the product of a cross between several other breeds, most notably the bull dog and terriers. The dog was especially popular with butchers, and so it was referred to for a long time as the "butcher's dog." The breed originated in the central and eastern neighborhoods of Paris and became famous when one became the constant companion of Pierre MacOrlan.

This dog is easily recognizable by its small size, large, square head, short, pug-nosed face, and powerful, compact body. The coat is made of fur that is short, tight, shiny and soft. There are two types: one

PUG

with a black and red and sometimes white coat, the other white with black spots.

Seen here beside Claire Jacquet, and vigilant as ever, is Enny Idole de Livandy, known as Etienne. His attitude is characteristic of French bulldogs, who are devoted to their masters, very affectionate and extremely protective of children.

Could it be the rich history of this breed that makes Cupidon del Sol Lleban and Mr. and Mrs. Beretta so pensive? In the sixteenth century, Dutch sailors brought the dog back from China, where it was known to the Chinese as the "Paï." They offered several dogs to William I the Taciturn, *stathouder* of the United Provinces. He took them wherever he went—a lucky thing as they saved his life by alerting him to an imminent attack by Spanish assassins in 1573. The royal family of Orange-Nassau was so appreciative that William III of Orange brought the dog with him to England when he was crowned sovereign in 1689. To own a pug became a status symbol among the

nobles who, unfortunately, deliberately limited the numbers of this breed. It wasn't until the success of the Franco-British Chinese expedition of 1860 that the dog started to be imported regularly, which led to a spectacular growth in its popularity during the nineteenth century. Fortune turned, however, on the pug at the beginning of the twentieth century when the terrier became the new breed of fashion. Following World War II, the duke and duchess of Windsor showed up habitually at social functions accompanied by their pugs, which resulted in the breed's regained popularity.

This is a small, compact dog with a large, heavy-set and round head. The eyes are large and prominent

with a lively expression. The ears are small. The tail is rolled up tight on the hindquarters, and the coat is colored silver, apricot, beige or black. Its black face earned the dog the nickname of "Carlin" in France and Italy in honor of a popular eighteenth-century Italian actor whose first name was Carlo, and who was famous for the black mask he always wore on stage. The Germans and the Dutch call the dog "Mops" (wrathful) due to its fierce-looking head.

The pug, however, is a friendly, outgoing dog who loves to play. The English name "pug" comes from the dog's small size.

HUNGARIAN GREYHOUND

The Hungarian greyhound has ancient Asiatic origins. It came to Europe with the first Magyars who settled near the Carpathian mountains in the ninth century. It was crossed with other greyhound breeds in the nineteenth century to enhance its speed and agility.

Less elongated than the standard greyhound, this dog also has a longer and more curved tail. The dog is about 28 inches tall, and the head is triangular in shape. The ears are of medium length and floppy. The neck is muscular, and the back is straight. The coat is composed of short fur and is slightly rough. The color of the coat can vary and is either uniformly spotted or even striped.

In 1987, Vera Arpadhazi was the first dog of her kind to have been imported to France. Mr. Chrisophe Carrier is especially fond of this dog as he initiated the first French Hungarian greyhound breeding program with her. He loves this breed for its athletic qualities and endurance. The dog is also known for its courage and discretion.

ARABIAN GREYHOUND

The Arabian greyhound descends from a primitive Asiatic greyhound. The dog was introduced into North Africa in the seventeenth century during the Arab conquest.

The development of the breed was initially rather haphazard, but a more homogenous line emerged with breeders who belonged to nomadic tribes. Its noble character so impressed the nomadic chiefs that they considered the dog worthy of a place among them in their tents.

Measuring 26 to 30 inches tall and weighing an average of 66 pounds, this dog has an elongated and elegant head. The back is short and almost horizontal, and the tail is very thin. The coat is so fine that the dog's wiry body is readily apparent. This quality is especially visible in D'Selma. Her aloofness might make you think that she prefers to ignore Mrs. Renée Lagrange, but this is hardly the case. Despite the seemingly haughty personality, this dog gets very attached to its masters, and albeit subtly, D'Selma is watching Mrs. Lagrange and is ready at all times to obey her every command.

SALUKI

This dog's ancestors were the large primitive Asiatic greyhounds that inhabited Central Asia some 10,000 years ago. The British discovered this Persian greyhound in the late nineteenth century and started breeding the dog in the early twentieth century. Breeding began in France after World War II. Bloody Grizzly de Cassandra, seen here in front of Miss Claudine Boyaval, epitomizes the characteristic grace and symmetry of this breed (above). The dog is 24 to 28 inches tall and weighs between 33 and 66 pounds. It has the perfect build for hunting. The elongated head features large floppy ears covered with silky fur. The tail is long and well-furnished with tassels. The coat is smooth and soft and can be white, beige, golden, red, gray and tan, black and tan, or black, white and tan. This is a faithful, friendly and dignified dog.

IRISH WOLFHOUND

What an incredible impression Epahaistos of Leanan Sidhe and Dew of Leanan Sidhe make. Mr. Bridier's dogs epitomize the perfectly controlled power of this breed (right). But also note their serenity and gentleness. The breed is descended from wirehaired Continental greyhounds that date to the early Christian era. From the tenth to the seventeenth centuries, the Irish wolfhound was used to hunt wolves. Standing 36 inches tall and weighing around 175 pounds, this is, along with the Great Dane, the largest dog breed. These dogs are strongly built and muscular yet agile. The head and tail are carried high. The wiry coat can be gray, red, black or white. This is also a good guard dog, and its imposing size can be very dissuasive.

SCOTTISH DEERHOUND

Mistic-Myth of the Funny Hill, who belongs to Mrs. Duval-Pinset, is a charming companion (following two pages).

The name deerhound points to the fact that this large dog (29 inches) descends from primitive greyhounds that accompanied the Celts when they settled in Scotland around 300 B.C. This dog was a formidable deerhunter and was perfect for hunting in the forests that cover the Scottish Highlands. The Scottish deerhound has a long, flat head. The muzzle is narrow and tapered at the nose. The neck is long and the shoulders angular. The long tail hangs straight down when the dog is at rest. The coat is wiry and coarse and about 4 inches long. The coat is longer around the head, the chest and the stomach. It can be gray-blue (the most sought-after color), light gray or spotted gray.

GREYHOUND

This dog's ancestors were primitive greyhounds that arrived with the Celts when they settled in the British Isles. During the Middles Ages, this hunting dog was restricted to the nobility, who alone had the right to hunt. Later, when the right to hunt was extended to the population at large, hunting competitions became so popular that certain breeders crossed the greyhound with the bull terrier. It was at this point that the standard breed was established as it exists today. The greyhound is 28 to 30 inches tall. It has a long head and a long tail. Its broad, elevated chest and elongated neck, along with its long, square back account for the harmonious and aerodynamic shape of this dog. The fur is tight and fine. The coat can be uniformly black, white, red, blue, or fawn, or it can have any mixture of those colors offset with white. At one time a deerhunting dog, the greyhound has remained to this day an inveterate hunting dog. Its speed and endurance are remarkable.

Mr. Labastrou belongs to a family that has always been fond of the greyhound breeds. He is very attached to Danton du Lavoir de Datchet, a superb athlete and the very symbol, in his eyes, of loyalty.

WHIPPET

This small English greyhound has distant origins, despite the fact that its name didn't appear until the nineteenth century. Its defining characteristics were not established until the late nineteenth century when the breed was crossed with fox terriers. The characteristics were further developed following an intensive breeding program based on the dog's ability to compete in the ever popular dog races. The head is long, with small ears. The chest is considerably elevated; the back is rather wide and long, and the tail is tapered. The fur is short, fine and very tight, and the coat can be any color.

Emil du Manoir de la Grenouillère, shown here at the feet of Mrs. Jackie Bourdin (right), is surrounded by four whippets. The whippet is a hunting dog with astonishing acceleration and stamina. When in action, the dog tends to straighten up its ears. Mrs. Bourdin's whippets are regular participants in dog racing competitions. Below is Oakbark Master Quiz, who belongs to Mr. Alain Olu.

SPANISH GREYHOUND

The Romans introduced Celtic greyhounds into Spain, and later the conquering Arabs imported Asiatic greyhounds. The Spanish greyhound is the product of several crosses between these earlier breeds. After deciding that the breed lacked sufficient speed, it was crossed with the standard greyhound, and the result was the modern Spanish greyhound. Today, it is used to hunt wild hare in Spain, where the use of greyhounds for hunting is not forbidden. The dog is also used in hunting rabbit and fox.

The dog stands 26 to 28 inches tall at the shoulder and weighs around 66 pounds. The head is long, and straight with large nostrils and trian-

gular ears. The back is long, and the stomach is arched. Its long tail ends in a point. The coat can be any color, but the most common colors are fawn and brindled or black. The breed is divided into two categories, distinguished by the nature of their coats. The first type has a coarse, semi-long coat, as can be seen on

Vasconcico, called Vasco (black), and Vilancico, called Vivaldi (brindled), both of whom belong to Mr. Pierre Faure (right). Having coats typical of the breed, both of these dogs exemplify the breed's excellent balance, which comes from regular exercise and chasing decoys.

Vincanilla, called Vinca, belongs to

Mr. Claude Berger and is the second type of Spanish greyhound (below). His beautiful brindled coat is made of short, tight fur that is smooth and shiny. Vinca, sitting here calmly beside Mr. Berger's daughter, Laetitia Gesret, demonstrates another outstanding quality of the breed—its unfailing obedience.

ITALIAN GREYHOUND

Sometime around 3000 B.C., the ancestors of the Italian greyhound enjoyed a privileged place among the Egyptians, who succeeded in miniaturizing a primitive Asiatic greyhound to create the breed. The P.L.I., as the French refer to the dog, was brought to Italy from Egypt and became a favorite among the Italian nobility. It was there that breeding programs established the modern breed. The search for perfection and refinement that so characterized the Renaissance was applied with equal enthusiasm to the breeding of this dog.

With its small size, the Italian greyhound is an active and energetic athlete, whose gait is characterized

by remarkably long strides. The dog is a model of grace and elegance, but it is also a wonderful companion, with an attractive and playful temperament. The head is tapered, and the muzzle is pointed. The ears are small and elegant. Its large eyes are very expressive. The coat is made of short hair that is glossy and soft to the touch, and it can be uniformly colored black, gray, fawn and beige, with a patch of white on the chest or at the end of the paws in some dogs.

A track champion, Ever Black de Shirkan and his admiring entourage belong to Mrs. Evelyne Diacquenod, who fondly remembers Ever Black's mother, Belle Bressane de Shirkan. She was a resolutely independent dog who would pass by the florist 's every day to say hello, after which she would return home for a quick nap. Then she would visit the TV store and the diner to say hello, before stopping at the butcher's where she knew the door would always be open. There she would lie down and wait patiently until Mrs. Diacquenod came to fetch her when the butcher called to say that Belle had arrived. Without even realizing it, Belle Bressane put into practice a sensible and widely employed political dictum: independence through interdependence.

BORZOÏ

The origins of this breed remain controversial, but it seems likely that the lineage of the borzoi includes diverse Asiatic greyhounds. The breed was more or less established in its modern form in the fifteenth century during the reign of Ivan the Terrible. The original breeders wanted a greyhound that would hunt wolves. That meant a large, strong and fast dog. The borzoi fit the bill perfectly.

The dog can be as tall as 33 inches and has a brilliant, silky, wavy coat that can be white and fawn, white and brindled, or black and white. Its large, somber, almond-shaped eyes accentuate the noble aspect of its long, chiseled head. Its back forms a long sloping arch, and its long tail is fringed.

Over time, this dog has become more of a pet than a hunting dog, yet it still retains many of the qualities for which it was originally bred. When given the occasion, this dog can be an avid and courageous hunter. These dogs can be intolerant and mistrustful of strange dogs but are real team players when it comes to those it knows. Such is the case with Dutka de la Polianka (white and fawn) and Kiev de la Polianka (black and white), who belong to Mrs. Pélisson. When one gets up and goes galloping off, the other immediately follows.

AZAWAKH

This elegant greyhound comes from the plateau of central Mali and was named for the Azawakh river. It arrived there in the eighth century with the people of the Saharas who were moving westward to escape the invading Arabs.

The dog is 30 inches tall and has a long, finely featured head with flat, floppy ears. The legs of this dog are long and thin, the chest is substantial, the back is straight and the tail is thin. The fur is short, fine and soft and forms a coat that varies from sandy white to brown. This is a generally slender dog, so slender, in fact, that its muscles and bones are readily visible through the coat. Judging by the proud, almost imperial appearance adopted by Cassque d'Or des Nomades Bleus, who belongs to Mrs. Françoise Heidmann, it is easy to see why the nomads of the Sahara considered the Azawakh to be an animal of ceremonial and ritual importance.

Acknowledgements

I would like to extend special thanks to Sylvie Mignon of the Central Canine Society who patiently answered our many questions concerning dogs and dog owners; Pierre de Mascureau, Director of the Central Canine Society; the presidents of all the dog clubs in France and their supporters, who are too numerous to mention individually; the techicians who set up the studio where the photographs were taken; the carpenters from Marcel Duperche's firm; the masons from the firm of Yves Cojean; the electricians from Flèche and Morin; and Willy Décor for their work on the interiors.

I would also like to thank my two assistants, Françoise Jacquot, who took care of scheduling, and Marc Lavaud, who was responsible for lighting, as well as Jean-Philippe Piter.

The film was developed in the GT3P laboratory at Saint-Remy-l'Honoré. The negatives were printed for the book by Rush Labo of Paris, who also handled the project presentation.

The photographs were made with a Mamiya RZ 67 and a Canon Eos 1 using a Godard flash.

Thanks also to the entire Sotexi team, particularly Giselle Nicot. The Kodak Ektachrome 100 X photos are distributed by Yann Arthus-Bertrand. Fax: (1) 45 66 52 05.

Artistic direction: Philippe Pierrelée, who was assisted by Sophie Domenach. Editorial office: Laurence Basset

316

INDEX

Original title: CHIENS
Written by: Andre Pittion-Rossillon
Photographs by: Yann Arthus-Bertrand
Art Direction: Philippe Pierrelée,
assisted by Sophie Domenach
Editor: Laurence Basset
Published by Les Editions du Chêne - Hachette Livre 1992
© 1993, Société nouvelle des Editions du Chêne

English editor: Lisa Davidson
Translator: John Herrick
Copyright © 2000 Editions du Chêne - Hachette Livre.
All rights reserved.
This edition published by Barnes & Noble, Inc.,
by arrangement with les Editions du Chêne.
© 2000 Barnes & Noble Books
M10987654321
ISBN : 0.7607.2218.8